The Wind at Work

An Activity Guide to Windmills

SECOND EDITION

Gretchen Woelfle

CHICAGO
REVIEW
PRESS

Copyright © 1997, 2013 by Gretchen Woelfle
All rights reserved
Second edition
Published by Chicago Review Press Incorporated
814 North Franklin Street
Chicago, Illinois 60610
ISBN 978-1-61374-100-9

Library of Congress Cataloging-in-Publication Data
Is available from the Library of Congress.

Cover design: Joan Sommers Design
Cover images: (clockwise from upper right) *The Mill at Wijk* by Jacob van Ruisdael,
    Royal Netherlands Embassy; wind farm, iStockphoto; wind turbine, iStockphoto;
    North American windmill, photograph by Bob Popeck
Interior design: Sarah Olson

Printed in the United States of America
5 4 3 2 1

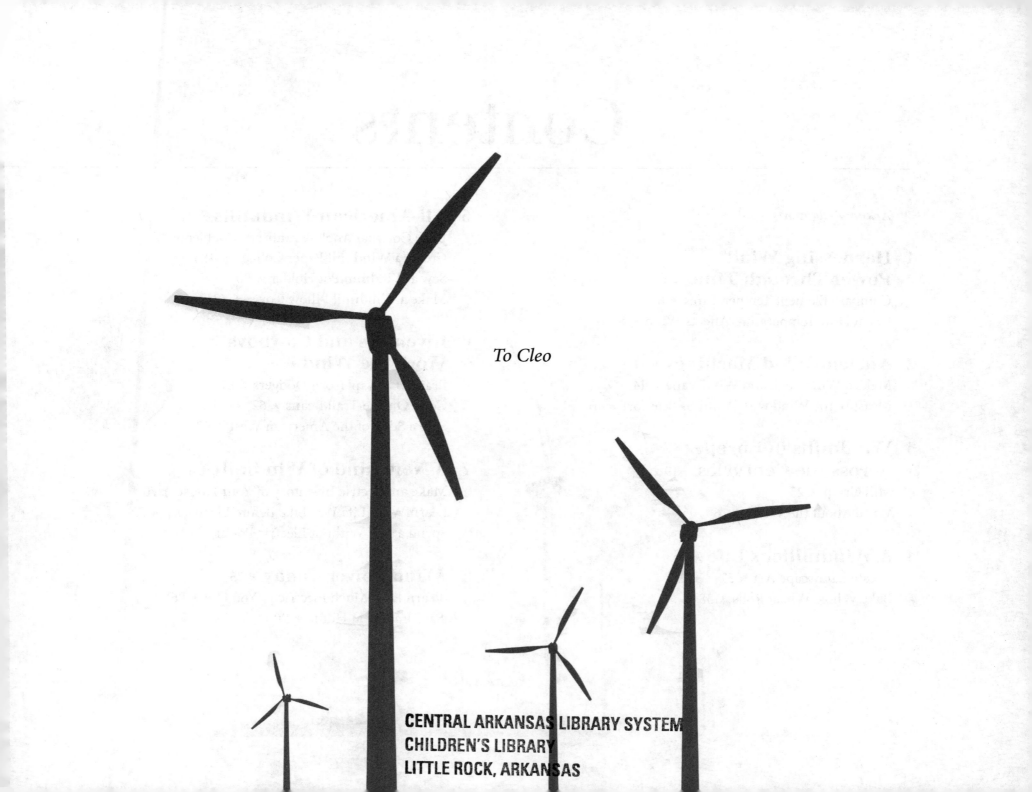

To Cleo

Contents

Acknowledgments ⋆ vii

1 **Harnessing Wind Power Through Time** ⋆ 1
Compare Element Temperatures ⋆ 6
Learn How Temperature Affects Wind ⋆ 8

2 **Ancient Wind Machines** ⋆ 11
Make a Wind Sock and Wind Vane ⋆ 14
Measure the Wind with Admiral Beaufort ⋆ 16

3 **Windmills in Europe Across the Centuries** ⋆ 19
Mill Grain ⋆ 25
Write About the Wind ⋆ 26

4 **A Windmiller's Life** ⋆ 29
Create Landscape Art ⋆ 37
Bake Whole Wheat Rolls ⋆ 38

5 **All-American Windmills** ⋆ 41
Bake Colonial Apple-Cranberry Cobbler ⋆ 47
Create a Windmill Paper Collage ⋆ 48
Sew a Windmill Pot Holder ⋆ 50
Make a Windmill Pillow Cover ⋆ 52

6 **Inventors and Cowboys Work the Wind** ⋆ 55
Prairie Cookin' Corn Dodgers ⋆ 61
Cook On-the-Trail Beans ⋆ 62
Sing a Song of the American West ⋆ 63

7 **A New Kind of Windmill** ⋆ 65
Make an Electric Inventory of Your House ⋆ 70
Learn What Life Was Like Before Electricity ⋆ 72
Spend a Day Without Electric Power ⋆ 73

8 **Wind Power Today** ⋆ 75
Learn How Much Electricity You Use ⋆ 86
Save Energy at Home ⋆ 90

9 A Solution in the Wind ⋆ 93

Find Out About Your Energy Sources ⋆ 102

Take Environmental Action ⋆ 103

10 Fulfilling the Promise ⋆ 105

Global Wind Day ⋆ 112

Investigate a Wind Farm ⋆ 113

Where to Find Windmills ⋆ 115

Resources ⋆ 123

Renewable Energy and Wind Energy Groups ⋆ 123

Student Environmental Groups ⋆ 123

Historical Associations ⋆ 124

Windmill Careers ⋆ 125

Glossary ⋆ 127

Picture Key to Windmills ⋆ 130

Bibliography ⋆ 133

Websites ⋆ 133

Books ⋆ 133

Author Interviews ⋆ 134

Source Notes ⋆ 134

Index ⋆ 137

Acknowledgments

As I sat down to write this second edition of *The Wind at Work*, I had a new tool to use—the Internet. It's hard to fathom that when I wrote the first edition back in the mid-1990s, I did all my research in books, corresponded by US Mail, found windmill sites via long-distance telephone calls, and collected illustrations printed on paper.

However, one source of information has remained the same—the generous people who provided information, research leads, photographs, and interviews. Paul Gipe was there in 1997 to help with the first edition, and he repeated the favor for this one. Dr. T. Lindsay Baker, still publishing the *Windmillers Gazette*, also helped. Dan Juhl of Juhl Wind, Inc.; Richard Miller of Hull, Massachusetts, Municipal Light Plant; Michael Wheeler of enXco; and Peggy McCoy of the Cascade Community Wind Project shared their time and experience. Kit Gray was a master of all things photographic. Alice Woelfle-Erskine proved an invaluable research assistant, and Cleo Woelfle-Erskine, writer and scientist, gave the book an astute reading as he himself works to heal the planet. Finally, Cynthia Sherry and her staff at Chicago Review Press deserve a big shout-out for keeping the first edition of *The Wind at Work* in print for 15 years and for overseeing its latest version. My thanks to them all.

1
Harnessing Wind Power Through Time

Night fell on the flatlands of Holland. The **wind** howled, rain slashed to earth, and waves broke higher and higher on the beach. Flashes of lightning revealed a high wall of earth built to hold back the sea. Waves crashed against this **dike**, throwing water to the fields beyond and washing away parts of the dike itself.

The Dutch called the sea the Waterwolf, and tonight the Waterwolf was on the prowl, trying to steal their lands. All night long flickering lanterns moved along the top of the dike as villagers kept watch. If the dikes broke, the Waterwolf would swallow their farms and homes.

By morning, the rain subsided and the wind dropped. The storm was over. The dikes had held. Tired Dutchmen stumbled home to bed.

But there was no rest for the **windmillers**. All night they had worked the **windmills** to pump water from the overflowing canals back out to sea. Now they had to drain the flooded fields to save the crops. For days and nights, giant **windmill sails** would turn, pumping and pumping until the fields were dry. The wind that nearly destroyed the land would now help to save it.

The History of Wind Power

Wind is created by the sun as it warms the earth unevenly. Warm air expands and rises. Cool air rushes in to take its place. This air movement is what we call the wind.

For more than a thousand years people have harnessed the wind with windmills. People used the wind to propel sailboats on the water long before they built windmills on land. Billowing sails filling with wind replaced the hard work of men rowing and paddling. Eventually, wind-powered machines moved on land and saved a lot of heavy labor. The wind-filled windmill sails then turned a shaft, wheels, gears, and finally, **millstones**, water pumps, or other machines. Before the invention of windmills and water mills, men or animals turned heavy millstones by trudging around and around in a circle, hour after hour, day after day, crushing grain to make flour. It was mind-numbing, body-breaking work.

The wind is not a perfect source of energy. It can be steady or gusty. It can change direction in a few seconds. It can grow to the force of a hurricane or die completely. Scientists can predict daily and seasonal wind patterns, but these patterns won't tell if or how much the wind will blow tomorrow afternoon. Even so, the wind has been reliable enough for many uses through the centuries.

Rembrandt van Rijn (1609–1669), one of the Netherlands' greatest artists, was the son of a windmiller. He grew up across the street from his father's malt mill in Leyden. The mill stood on the banks of the Rhine River (spelled "Rijn" in Dutch). The family took this name for their own. Here Rembrandt portrays a smock mill and the miller's house next door.
Rijksmuseurn-Stichting, Amsterdam

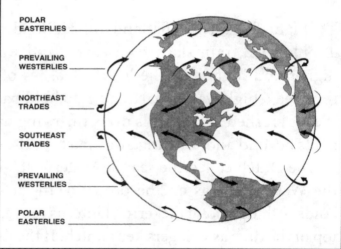

Wind is created by the sun as it warms the earth unevenly. Lands near the equator get more sun than those near the poles. Summer brings more sun than winter. Warm air expands and rises, and cool air rushes in to take its place. The drawing shows the usual, or prevailing, winds in different parts of the earth. *Kristin Brivchik*

B. *Brake mechanism:* Mechanism to stop the sails from turning.

C. *Windshaft:* The axle on which the sails are mounted.

This cutaway drawing of a windmill shows different parts of the machinery in a grist (grinding) mill.

Bruce Loeschen

F. *Sack lift:* Rope is wound around this wooden drum, which pulls sacks of grain to the third level of the mill.

J. *Sack trap:* Portion of the floor that opens, allowing millers to pull up sacks of grain to the third level.

L. *Grindstones or millstones:* Always in pairs, the bottom stone is stationery and is called the bed stone. The top stone revolves and is called the runner stone.

A. *Brake wheel:* Cogwheel mounted on the windshaft that drives the wallower, and around the rim of which the brake contracts to stop the mill.

D. *Wallower:* The large circle with cogs that turns the main shaft.

E. *Main shaft:* The main upright driving shaft.

G. *Great spur wheel:* The main driving wheel for millstones and other power wheels.

H. *Cogwheel:* Meshes with smaller cogwheels that drive other millstones and machinery.

I. *Grain chute:* Guides grain into hopper.

K. *Hopper:* Placed above the vat that holds the grain waiting to be ground.

(left) Along the seacoast the land and the air above the land warm up quicker than the water. All day long this warm air rises and cool sea breezes blow from the ocean to the land.

Kristin Brivchik

(right) In the evening the land cools off quicker, and the ocean remains warmer. Warm ocean air rises and a cooler land breeze blows out to sea.

Kristin Brivchik

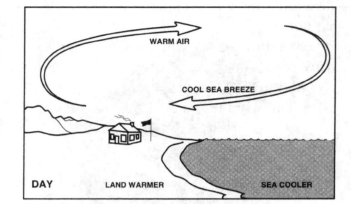

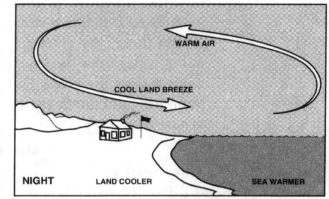

The Mill at Wijk by Dutch artist Jacob van Ruisdael (1628–1682). The 1600s were the golden age of Dutch windmills and landscape painting.
Royal Netherlands Embassy

Like the wind itself, windmills have come and gone. From AD 1200 to 1900, windmills were the most powerful machines in Europe. They ground grain, pumped water, pressed oil, sawed wood, and performed many other tasks. In the 1800s windmills were replaced by steam engines. Today about 900 Dutch windmills remain out of 10,000 that stood 200 years ago. In America, six million windmills pumped water on the dry Western plains until the 1940s, when electric and gasoline engines did away with most of them. Today a new kind of windmill turns in the wind.

Many people think of Dutch models when they think of windmills, but windmills come in many shapes and sizes. Ancient Persian-style mills looked like revolving doors. Modern **wind turbines** look like giant airplane propellers. All of them can harness a powerful energy source to work for us.

Wind Power Today

Thousands of wind turbines stand in the hills and plains of the United States today. Thousands more are scattered across Canada, Europe, China, and the rest of the world. They are new versions of an old idea.

From far away, wind turbines look like toy pinwheels that catch the sunlight as they spin. Up close, these pinwheel giants stand on 300-foot towers with whirling blades up to 300 feet in diameter. A generator behind the blades converts wind energy to electricity. Underground cables carry electric currents to power lines that feed the electricity to nearby towns and cities.

Clean, Renewable Energy Source

Wind power is a renewable source of energy, so we will never run out of it. It's clean, safe, and free for all to use.

Currently, most of the energy we use comes from burning coal, oil, and natural gas. These are called **fossil fuels**. When these fuels burn, gases such as carbon dioxide, nitrogen oxides, and sulfur compounds escape into the air. The gases react with sunlight to create smog. They also trap heat in our atmosphere and cause **global warming**. All these conditions are harmful to forests, crops, wildlife, and humans.

Wind power is a clean, economical energy source that can help reduce environmental pollution. Wind turbines could generate 20 percent of America's electrical power by the year 2030. This would reduce carbon emissions by an amount equal to what 140 million cars produce each year. Wind power is a clean, **renewable energy** that we will never use up. Some people discovered this a thousand years ago. Others don't know about it yet. But whether you've heard it or not, there's good news in the wind.

These Southern California wind turbines stand on the site of one of the first wind farms in the world. Larger, more efficient turbines have replaced earlier models, and today you can see wind turbines like these generating electricity all around the world. *Iberdrola Renewables*

José Mascurel and his family pose proudly near the windmill on their ranch in Hollywood, California, in the 1880s. *Seaver Center for Western History Research, Los Angeles County Museum of Natural History*

COMPARE ELEMENT TEMPERATURES

Goal: *Understand temperature patterns that affect the wind.*

Materials

* 2 plastic buckets of the same size
* Garden soil
* Water
* 3 outdoor thermometers
* Notebook
* Pencil
* Sheet of graph paper
* 3 markers of different colors
* Ruler

Directions

Fill one bucket with garden soil and the other bucket with water. Place a thermometer in each bucket. Place the buckets side by side outdoors. Place the third thermometer on the ground nearby to measure the air temperature. Make sure you place the buckets and thermometers where the sun can shine on them for part of each day.

Use the notebook to record your observations three times a day. For each observation, record the day of the week, the time of day, the name of the element (water, garden soil, or air), the temperature reading on the thermometer, and the weather conditions. Record your observations for three days.

DAY	TIME	ELEMENT	TEMPERATURE	CONDITION
Monday	morning	water	76 degrees	sunny with clouds
Monday	morning	soil	78	same
Monday	morning	air	77	same
Monday	afternoon	water	82	sunny
and so on . . .				

At the end of your three days of observation, create a chart on a sheet of graph paper like the one shown on the next page. Write in a temperature range on the vertical axis and the days on the horizontal axis, leaving enough room to record your three daily observations. Use a different color marker to record your observations for each element. Place a dot in the spot where the day of the week and time intersect with the recorded temperature. Once you've recorded all your observations, use a ruler to connect these dots.

Results

What element has the highest temperature—water, garden soil, or air—in the morning? Afternoon? Evening?

Which element heats up the most during the day?

Which element cools down the most at night?

Which element shows the least temperature change during the day?

What does this tell you about the relative temperature of the oceans, earth, and atmosphere?

How might these temperature differences affect wind patterns?

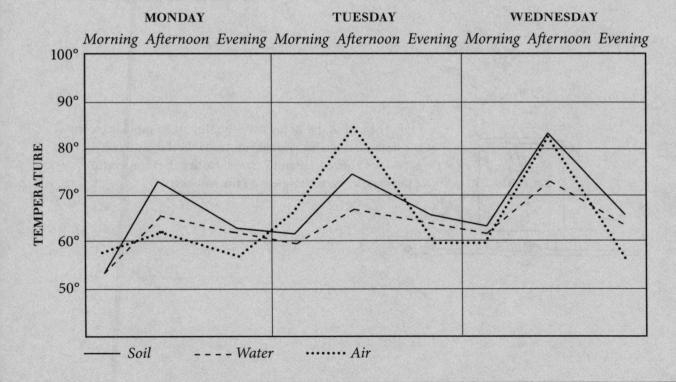

LEARN HOW TEMPERATURE AFFECTS WIND

Goal: *Observe the flow of air in warm and cool environments.*

Adult supervision required

Materials

* 2-foot piece of aluminum foil
* Small piece of modeling clay
* Thick candle, 4 inches tall
* Matchbook
* 2 small wooden blocks, 1 or 2 inches thick
* Empty soup can, with label and both ends removed
* Sharp knife
* Piece of heavy cotton string, 3 inches long (don't use nylon string!)

Directions

Spread the aluminum foil on top of a table. Secure the candle to the foil with clay. Light the candle. Place 2 wooden blocks on opposite sides of the candle. Carefully place the can over the candle and resting on top of the 2 blocks. The candle flame should not show above the can. (If the candle is too tall, blow it out and cut it at the bottom with a sharp knife so it will fit inside the can.)

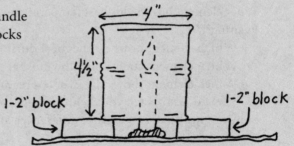

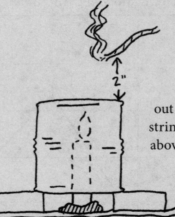

Light the end of the string over the sink, then quickly blow out the flame. The string should smoke. Hold the smoking string 2 inches above the candle flame. Notice the temperature above the candle. What happens to the smoke?

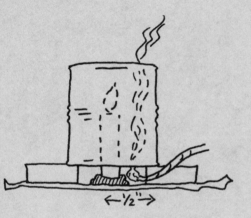

While the string continues to smoke, hold it beside the candle, about a foot away. Notice the temperature now. What happens to the smoke?

Finally, hold the string near the table top, about ½ inch from the edge of the can. What happens to the smoke? How can you explain this?

Results

If our atmosphere were all the same temperature, air wouldn't move. However, sunlight warms our atmosphere just like a candle warms the air around it. The warm air rises, and the cooler air moves in to take its place. So, when you hold the string directly above the candle, the smoke rises. When you hold the string a foot away from the heat source, the smoke drifts because the air surrounding the string is not as warm. Finally, when you hold the string close to the bottom of the tin can, the smoke is drawn up under the can and rises because the smoke moves in the direction of the warmer air.

2

Ancient Wind Machines

Before people invented windmills they found other ways to harness the wind. Sails on boats carried mariners faster and farther than before. Four thousand years ago men in large sailing canoes explored the South Pacific. They found their way by watching the wind, stars, and ocean currents as they sailed from one small island to another across hundreds of miles of open ocean. In Egypt, graceful **dhows** have sailed down the Nile River for 5,000 years. By 450 BC Phoenician sailors had traveled beyond the Mediterranean, north to Britain and south along the west coast of Africa.

Kites in the Wind

Kites are another way that the wind has been used for exploration. More than 2,000 years ago, the Chinese began flying kites. They flew them in battle to signal their troops. On Kite Day they sent kites aloft, asking the sky gods to send good fortune in the coming year.

Benjamin Franklin began experimenting with kites as a boy. One day he floated on his back while his kite pulled him more than a mile across a lake. Since his kite would not carry him back against the wind, he paid a smaller boy a few pennies to tote his clothes from one shore to another.

In 1752 Franklin flew a kite during a thunderstorm to prove that lightning contained electricity. He tied a key to the end of a silk kite string before sending it aloft. When lightning did strike his kite, he felt a slight electrical shock. He was lucky that his kite string remained fairly dry or his experiment would have been much more shocking. A Russian professor was killed a year later when he repeated Franklin's experiment with a wet kite string.

Scientists continued to use kites into the 1900s. Wilbur and Orville Wright designed and flew giant box kites. These experiments helped them invent the first successful airplane in 1903. From 1898 to 1933, the US Weather Service sent kites aloft to record temperature, humidity, and wind speed.

Wind Furnaces

Archaeologists in the early 1990s found evidence to suggest that people living in Sri Lanka in the AD 700s used the wind to smelt (separate) metal from rock ore in an unexpected way. Traditionally, smelting furnaces are tall, narrow structures. People fan the furnace with a **bellows** to make the fire burn very hot—hot enough to melt metal.

But in Sri Lanka they dug large crescents near the top of steep mountainsides. Each July and August monsoon winds blew across the Indian Ocean, up the slopes, and into these crescent-shaped furnaces. Winds of 25 to 30 mph rushed into the furnaces and created a mini-tornado. Charcoal fires inside the furnace reached at least 2200°F (1200°C), hot enough to smelt iron or steel.

Professor Gill Juleff, the British archaeologist in charge of the excavations, says, "These furnaces break all the rules about smelting furnaces, yet we're sure they were used for making iron, and perhaps steel." Muslim armies invaded Sri Lanka during that time, and iron and steel were probably used for weapons as well as farming tools.

Persian Windmills

We first hear of windmills from traveling Arab geographers around AD 950. They visited the high

(*left*) In 1752 Benjamin Franklin used a kite to prove that lightning contained a massive electrical charge.
Library of Congress Prints and Photographs USZ62-I433

(*right*) In the early 1900s, long before weather satellites circled the earth, the US Weather Service sent kites aloft to record temperature, humidity, and wind speed.
National Oceanic and Atmospheric Administration/Department of Commerce

desert plains of Seistan in ancient Persia, near the present Iran-Afghanistan border. There, a hot gale force wind blew from June through September. It was called "the wind of 120 days, the wind that killed cows."

People in Seistan built **vertical axis windmills** that resembled modern revolving doors enclosed on two sides. The wind entered on one side, twirled the doors around, and exited on the other side. Attached to millstones, the windmills ground corn into meal. Connected to a pump, they raised water from underground wells to irrigate the parched land. The advantage of this windmill was that it worked no matter which way the wind blew. However, the wind only pushed against one door at a time, so only one-fourth of the windmill was using the wind at any given moment.

Windmills on the Move

Legend has it that in the 1200s the Mongolian armies of Genghis Khan captured Persian windmill builders and took them to China to build irrigation windmills. Persian-style windmills also spread westward through the Middle East. In Egypt they were used to grind sugar cane.

Centuries later, European settlers in the West Indies hired Egyptians to plant sugar cane and build windmills to grind it. It was in this way that a few ancient Persian-style windmills reached the New World.

Around AD 950 the ancient Persians constructed a windmill by fastening bundles of reeds to a frame that rotated as the wind blew. They built walls around it to create a "wind tunnel" that would increase the force of the wind. *Sandia National Laboratory*

MAKE A WIND SOCK AND WIND VANE

Wind socks are used in airports to show which direction the wind is blowing.

Goal: *Make a wind sock and a* **wind vane** *and learn how they work.*

Adult supervision required

Materials

* Scissors
* Nylon knee sock or knee-high hose, 15 to 18 inches long
* 12-ounce Styrofoam cup
* Pencil
* ³⁄₁₆-inch wooden dowel, 3 feet long
* Masking tape
* 1 pushpin
* ¼-inch washer
* 2 straight plastic straws, 8 inches long (not the flexible kind)
* Ruler
* Sheet of construction paper
* White glue
* Compass

Directions

Wind Sock

Use the scissors to cut off the toe of the sock or the knee-high hose so that it is open at each end.

Using scissors, cut out the bottom of the Styrofoam cup. With a sharp pencil, bore a hole in the cup, just below the raised rim. This hole should be big enough for the ³⁄₁₆-inch dowel to fit through. Bore another hole directly opposite the first one.

Stretch the wide end (knee end) of the sock or hose over the bottom of the cup up to the raised rim. Tape the sock or hose onto the rim by securing it with one long piece of tape. Reinforce it with four small pieces of tape around the rim.

Use scissors to snip holes in the sock or hose where the cup holes are located.

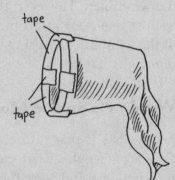

Wind Sock Pole

Push the pushpin through the top end of the dowel as far as it will go. Then twist and remove the pushpin. (This hole will be needed for the next stage, when you make your wind vane.)

Slide the wind sock onto the dowel through the two holes, leaving 1 inch free at the top.

Slide the ¼-inch washer up the pole until it rests just below the Styrofoam cup. Wrap a piece of tape around the pole several times just underneath the washer until it is thick enough to hold the washer in place. The washer will prevent the wind sock from sliding down the pole.

Wrap another strip of tape around the top end of the dowel just above the wind sock to keep it from sliding off the top of the pole.

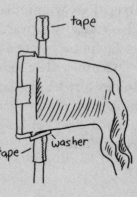

Wind Vane

Carefully cut a ¼-inch slit in each end of the straws. Cut four small 1-by-l-inch squares of construction paper. Mark each square of construction paper with compass direction N, S, E, or W. Dab a drop of white glue on each side of the paper and slip a piece into each slit on the ends of the straws. Place N and S on the two ends of one straw, and E and W on the ends of the other straw, just like the compass points. Be sure that the paper is horizontal. Dab more glue on the spots where the paper meets the straw to secure. Allow this to dry.

Measure the straws and find the middle of each. Pierce the middle of each straw with the pushpin. Then dab the following surfaces with white glue: the top of the dowel with the pushpin hole, the middle of each straw, and the point of the pushpin.

Insert the pushpin through both straws and into the top of the dowel. Be certain the straws form a cross, with the arms forming 90-degree angles. Wipe off excess glue. Allow glue to dry before trying the experiments.

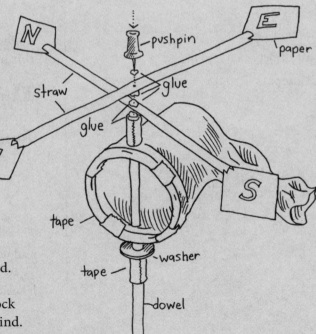

Experiment

Take your wind sock outside and watch it fill with wind. Wind speed increases with altitude, so use the highest (safe) location you can find to test your wind sock. Walk to the top of a nearby hill or climb to the top of the slide on a playground. If you can't find any place higher than the level ground, hold the wind sock above your head. Try to stay clear of trees and buildings. These will block the wind.

Use a compass to find north. Point your N straw vane in that direction. Your wind sock will turn until it faces into the wind. The wind vane will show you the direction of the wind.

In the next activity, you can use your wind sock to determine how fast the wind is blowing.

MEASURE THE WIND WITH ADMIRAL BEAUFORT

Young Francis Beaufort joined the British Royal Navy and went to sea when he was 12 years old. For more than 20 years he learned the ways of the wind. In 1805 he devised a scale to determine the wind speed by looking at things around him—trees, flags, smoke. In later years he became Admiral Sir Francis Beaufort. Today, sailors, meteorologists, and others continue to rely on the Beaufort scale. You can find the wind speeds in your neighborhood by using your wind sock and wind vane from the previous activity and by following the Beaufort scale.

Goal: Observe and measure wind patterns at different times of the day. Calibrate (adjust) your wind sock and wind vane to the Beaufort scale.

Materials

* Wind sock and wind vane (see "Make a Wind Sock and Wind Vane" activity on page 14)
* Notebook
* Pencil
* Beaufort scale (see page 17)
* Compass

Experiment

Take your wind sock to your backyard, school yard, or a nearby park. Find an open area, away from trees and buildings. Observe the wind in the same place in the morning, afternoon, and evening for five days. Watch how the wind moves different things: the tops of trees, a tall flagpole, your wind sock. Using the Beaufort scale, estimate the wind speed and record it in your notebook.

Recopy the Beaufort scale in your notebook but leave room to record your own observations under the description column. Observe how your wind sock reacts to different wind speeds. Add this information to the description column on your Beaufort scale.

Find north using your compass. Point the N arm of your wind vane north. Find the wind direction using your wind sock and record it in your notebook.

Results

You will probably memorize the Beaufort scale after a few days and then you'll always know how hard the wind is blowing! How could this be useful to you?

When does the wind blow strongest in your neighborhood? When is it weakest? Do you notice any wind-speed pattern?

Try this experiment during different seasons. Do you see the same wind patterns in summer and winter? In the rainy season and the dry season?

What sort of geographical area do you live in—plains, valley, mountains, desert, seaside, or lakeside? How does this help to explain the wind patterns you find?

BEAUFORT SCALE

BEAUFORT NUMBER	NAME OF WIND	SIGNS/DESCRIPTION	WIND SPEED (MPH)
0	calm	calm; smoke rises vertically	<1
1	light air	smoke drifts, indicating wind direction	1–3
2	light breeze	wind felt on face; leaves rustle; flags stir	4–7
3	gentle breeze	leaves and small twigs in constant motion	8–12
4	moderate breeze	small branches move; wind raises dust and loose paper	13–18
5	fresh breeze	small-leaved trees begin to sway; crested wavelets form on inland water	19–24
6	strong breeze	overhead wires whistle; umbrellas difficult to control; large branches move	25–31
7	moderate gale or near gale	whole trees sway; walking against wind is difficult	32–38
8	fresh gale or gale	twigs break off trees; moving cars veer	39–46
9	strong gale	slight structural damage occurs such as signs and antennas blown down	47–54
10	whole gale or storm	trees uprooted; considerable structural damage occurs	55–63
11	storm or violent storm	widespread damage occurs	64–74*
12	hurricane	widespread damage occurs	>74

*The United States uses 74 mph as the speed criterion for a hurricane.

3
Windmills in Europe Across the Centuries

On the windy plains of Suffolk, along the east coast of England, a strange sight appeared one day in AD 1191. Dean Herbert, an old priest from the local church, built a windmill with two heavy millstones to grind wheat into flour for the people of the parish.

Abbot Samson, the head of the nearby monastery, heard about the new machine and ordered his workmen to tear it down. The abbot owned the only water mill in the region. Every farmer came to his mill to grind grain into flour to make his bread, and each of them gave the abbot a share of their flour as payment. A curious mill like Herbert's windmill was bound to attract a lot of customers. This would not do.

When poor Herbert learned of the abbot's objection and realized there was no way to change his mind, Herbert ordered his own workers to take the mill apart so that he could at least save the lumber. The abbot's men were shocked when they arrived at the location of Herbert's mill and found nothing but the wind.

Postmills

No one knows how windmills found their way to Europe. The Crusaders, European soldiers who tried to capture Palestine from the Turks, probably saw Persian-style windmills in the Middle East. However, the windmills that appeared in Europe were nothing like the Persian ones. Perhaps they were reinvented in Europe.

These earliest European windmills are called **postmills**. These mills resemble a type of water mill found in Europe around 1200. Some historians believe that a clever person turned a water mill upside down, enlarged its paddles to catch the wind, and invented the first postmill.

Millwrights built postmills out of wood, with a few iron fastenings. The mill had to be light enough for the miller to turn, yet strong enough to withstand the fiercest storms and constant vibrations caused by spinning sails and grinding gears.

The mill had to be perfectly balanced so that the millstones remained level no matter which way the mill was turned. If the stones weren't level, grain would not grind evenly. Many postmills lasted for centuries, thanks to the superb engineering skills of medieval millwrights.

Smock Mills

During the 1300s, one millwright realized that he didn't need to turn the entire postmill when the wind changed direction; he only needed to turn the sails. The sails, attached to the roof or cap of the mill, could revolve on an outdoor track. The miller turned only the cap to face the sails into the wind. The rest of the building remained fixed to the ground. This meant the mill could be bigger, heavier, and stronger. These mills reminded people of the long shirts, or smocks, that farmers wore, so they called them **smock mills**.

(left) Postmills had a square box called a buck that was built around a central post and set high on a revolving platform. Large wooden sails covered with cloth faced directly into the wind. When the wind changed direction, the miller climbed down a stairway at the back, then pushed a long pole to turn the windmill.
Rijksmuseum-Stichting, Amsterdam

(center) The sails are attached to the cap of this smock mill. The windmiller turned only the cap when the wind changed direction. The largest, heaviest windmills were smock mills.
Rijksmuseum-Stichting, Amsterdam

(right) This tall smock mill towers above the schooners docked along the Zaan River in the Netherlands.
Netherlands Board of Tourism

Windmills in Southern Europe

In the 1500s people in Spain, Greece, and the Mediterranean islands began to build small stone **tower windmills**. In these drier countries, windmills were used to pump water to irrigate fields as well as to grind grain. There are 10 restored tower windmills in Campo de Critana, La Mancha, Spain, that are now Cultural Heritage Sites.

Draining the Netherlands

"God created the world, but the Dutch created Holland," says an old Dutch proverb. The official name of the country is the Netherlands, which means "low lands," for much of the country is near or below sea level. For thousands of years the Dutch built sea walls, or dikes, to hold back the sea, their fierce Waterwolf.

In the 1600s the Dutch began to reclaim land that was below sea level. Using dikes and **drainage windmills**, they pumped water out of the lakes and marshes. As the new land dried, they dug canals to channel rainwater and groundwater for the new farms and villages they built. These new lands were called **polders**. With the help of windmills and dikes, the Dutch were able to hold back the Waterwolf and create a country that is twice as big as before.

Draining the English Fens

The English also tried to drain their marshes and create new farmland. In 1588 a drainage windmill began work in the **fens** (marshes) of Lincolnshire. Adventurers with money to spend hired drainers to do the work for them. But the fiercely independent **slodgers**, who lived by hunting and fishing

(*left*) This tower mill in Campo de Critana is one of the oldest windmills in Spain. Hundreds of similar ones dotted the country in past times. Though most of the old windmills are gone, the wind remains on the Spanish plains, turning the blades of wind turbines.

(*right*) In the rainy season, these windmills at the Kinderdijk in the Netherlands pump water from the fields, through the wide canals, and out to sea. In dry times, they pump water from the large canals to the fields. The flat land in the distance, called a polder, has been reclaimed from the sea.

Royal Netherlands Embassy

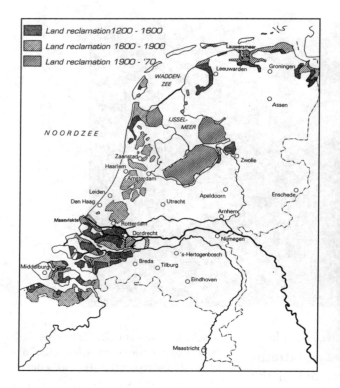

(*left*) This map of the Netherlands shows the area below sea level that has been pumped dry since AD 1200 to create new land, or polders. Until the mid-nineteenth century, this work was done by windmills. Tall earthen dikes throughout the Netherlands keep back the sea.

Information and Documentation Center for the Geography of the Netherlands

(*right*) Small mills, not much larger than a cow, pumped water in and out of irrigation canals in farm fields.

Seaver Center for Western History Research, Los Angeles County Museum of Natural History

in the fens, liked the land as it was. As soon as the drainers would build a dike and windmill, the slodgers tore it down. Nature was on the slodgers' side, for winter storms helped to destroy the dikes and flood the land again. The battle over the fens went on for centuries. It wasn't until the mid-1800s that the drainers finally won.

What Windmills Can Do

Windmills sprouted all over Europe and made many jobs easier and faster. By the early 1700s the Netherlands and England each had about 10,000 windmills. Thousands more worked in France, Germany, Denmark, and Eastern Europe.

Grist mills ground grain, but they also ground cocoa, gunpowder, malt, and mustard. **Paint mills** ground pigments for paint as well as herbs and chemicals to make medicines and poisons. **Oil mills** pressed the oil from seeds, and millers sold the leftover seedcakes for cattle feed. **Glue mills** processed cow hides and animal bones. **Hulling mills** removed the outer layer of rice and barley kernels. **Fulling mills** pounded woolen cloth into felt. The Dutch called these "stink mills," because rancid butter and aged urine were used in the process. Miners used windmills to blow fresh air into deep mine shafts. Windmills also provided power to make paper and to saw lumber.

Windmills came in all sizes. **Sawmills** with a crane, hoists, gears, and saws might be 80 feet tall with sails 100 feet in diameter. Large saw frames cut giant logs, and smaller saws cut beams and boards. Leftover scraps of lumber were sent to a small, 25-foot windmill that cut them into strips and slats. Many farms had even smaller mills, about five feet tall, to pump water from the fields.

Sawmills and paper mills grew so large—housing saws and pulp vats, storage and drying sheds—that they "split the seams" of their smock and became rectangular factories with windmills on top.

Windmill Opponents

Not everyone welcomed the new inventions. Dutch **guilds**—somewhat like our modern trade unions—protested against early industrial windmills, so the millers formed a guild of their own to promote their trade. In the 1600s English **sawyers** who were afraid of losing their jobs destroyed the first wind sawmill built in Deptford (near London).

In fact, windmills created new jobs. Because they drew on so much power, windmills needed many workers. In a paper mill, for example, wind turned machines that chopped rags, churned the chopped fiber into pulp, and ground scrap paper for recycling. The whole operation needed a miller to tend the windmill and workers to tear rags, fill the chopping and churning tubs, pour pulp into molds, hang paper up to dry, and then clean, press, and roll the paper until it was ready to be bound for shipment. Industries grew

quickly when mills harnessed the wind, but all the worried English sawyers in Deptford saw was an enormous machine stronger than their own muscle power.

Building a Better Windmill

As people thought up new uses for windmills, they also thought of ways to improve them. Englishman Edmund Lee invented the **fantail** in 1745. This was a round fan of small wind vanes mounted on the back of a windmill and connected to the track that ran around the cap. When the wind changed direction, the small fantail automatically swung around and moved the

Windmills gave jobs to many people. Even children worked in the paper mills, tearing rags that would be made into paper. Here a woman fills a tray with pulp in a paper mill. *De Zaansche Molen, Koog aan de Zaan, Netherlands*

large sails to face directly into the wind. There would be no more dashing outside in the freezing rain or a blustery gale to move the giant sails. The miller stayed inside and his fantail did the job for him. In 1759 England's John Smeaton discovered that twisting the sails about 20 degrees, like a modern airplane propeller, gave them more power. The sails caught hold of more wind and the mills worked faster.

In 1772, Scotsman Andrew Meikle invented a wooden sail that looked like a giant shutter or venetian blind. It was controlled by a spring set by the miller inside the mill. When the wind grew too strong, the shutters opened and slowed down the sails. England's Sir William Cubitt improved this idea in 1807 by introducing the **patent sail**, which used weights and counterweights to adjust the sails smoothly and steadily. Cloth sails spun faster, but patent sails were more automatic. British millers welcomed the new inventions, but the Dutch kept their old cloth sails.

When Napoleon and the French army invaded the Netherlands in 1806, they were astonished to see hundreds of grinding, sawing, pressing, and pumping windmills along the Zaan River just north of Amsterdam. Such a concentration of industrial power existed nowhere else in the world. Wind power had created the first Industrial Revolution in Europe.

MILL GRAIN

Dutch families used flour for pancakes, waffles, cookies, and porridge, but most of all for bread. They ate bread with each of their four meals—breakfast, dinner, mid-afternoon snack, and late-evening supper. Farm wives baked their own bread, but townsfolk bought bread from a baker. Both farm wives and bakers bought flour from the windmiller.

Goal: Grind grain by hand and experience the force needed to do the work of a windmill.

Materials

* A few handfuls of whole wheat berries (available at health food stores)
* 2 cement block bricks (2 by 3½ by 8 inches) or 1 cement block brick and a rough sidewalk
* Watch with second hand
* Dustpan
* Hand broom
* Measuring spoon (tablespoon)
* Bowl

Directions

Place a handful of whole wheat berries between two cement bricks or on a rough sidewalk. Place one brick on top of the berries and grind it by applying force in a back-and-forth motion. Time yourself. See how long it takes to grind the berries to a flourlike consistency. Is this as fine as the whole wheat flour you can buy in the store?

Sweep up the flour with a dustpan and hand broom. Use the measuring spoon to see how much whole wheat flour you've ground. Count the number of tablespoons you fill as you place your whole wheat flour in a bowl.

Grind one brick against the bare sidewalk. Then turn it over and feel the side that was grinding against the sidewalk. How does it feel? What might happen in a wooden windmill if the millstones rubbed together without grain in the middle?

If a Dutch family ate one loaf of bread at every meal and each loaf uses about 2 cups of flour, how many cups of flour would they use each day? How long would it take you to grind this much flour with your cement block bricks? (Hint: 16 tablespoons = 1 cup)

In chapter 4 we'll make some bread and taste how Dutch people enjoyed the results of the windmill's hard work.

WRITE ABOUT THE WIND

You can do these writing exercises alone or with a group of people, with everyone contributing words and ideas. If you work in a group, try writing your story, legend, or journal as a play with different people acting out each role.

Goal: *Use your imagination to experience the wind from different points of view and express this experience in words.*

Materials

* Pen or pencil
* Paper

Directions

Exercise 1: Imagine a Cool Wind on a Hot Day

Close your eyes and think about riding a bicycle, riding a skateboard, or roller skating on a hot, sunny day. What does the wind feel like blowing on your face? Think of words to describe this physical feeling. Open your eyes and write down your words.

Close your eyes again and get back on your imaginary bicycle, skateboard, or skates. Think of words to describe the sound of the wind. Open your eyes and write down your words. Repeat this process for seeing, tasting, and smelling the wind.

After you have compiled these lists of words describing the wind through your five senses, look at your list of words. Now write a paragraph or a poem using some of these words to describe exactly how you experienced the wind while on your bike, skateboard, or skates. (Hint: If you write a poem, try writing one that does not rhyme. You can choose from a greater variety of words this way.)

Read your paragraph or poem to someone else. Ask the person if he or she could feel the sensations about which you wrote.

Exercise 2: Imagine a Cold Wind in a Rainstorm

Repeat exercise 1 while you imagine walking against a strong wind on a cold, rainy afternoon. Close your eyes and imagine each of the following senses, one at a time: sound, touch, sight, taste, and smell. Write down your descriptive words for each sense. Choose the words that best describe walking through the cold, windy rainstorm and write a paragraph or poem about it. (Hint: Again, if you write a poem, try writing one that does not rhyme, so that you can choose from a greater variety of words.)

Read your paragraph or poem to someone else. Ask the person if he or she could feel the sensations about which you wrote.

Exercise 3: Write a Story About the Wind

Think of a friendly sort of wind that flies kites, pushes sailboats and windsurfers, makes waves on the water, pollinates plants, moves clouds across the sky, turns windmill sails, or makes the trees sway. Close your eyes and pretend you are a bird, a kite, a windmiller, a sailor, or a child lying on your back on the grass. A gentle wind is moving some of the things that surround you.

After a few minutes, open your eyes and begin writing a story by describing who you are, what you are doing, and what you see, hear, smell, taste, and touch. Remember that you are inventing a story with characters and a plot, not just writing a list of words.

Now imagine that the wind is growing stronger and stronger until it turns into a storm, a hurricane, or a tornado. Perhaps it starts raining or snowing or a raging wind sweeps a fire toward you. Think about what you might see, hear, smell, taste, or touch. (Remember, you are still a bird, sailor, child, or whatever you originally imagined.)

Write about what is happening around you now. You might use parts of a true experience or you might make up the whole story.

Now imagine that the wind finally dies down. What has happened to you? What has happened to the world around you? Write a conclusion to your story.

Read your story to another person. Ask the person if he or she could feel some of the same things that you wrote about in your story.

Exercise 4: Write a Legend About How the Wind Came to Be

Many cultures have legends about how the earth was made or how the first people were created. Think up a legend about how the wind came to be. Perhaps it resulted from an argument between the moon and the sun or the earth and the ocean. Perhaps the wind was the child of an unusual mother and father. Use your imagination and make your legend as fantastic as you like. Begin your story this way: *A long time ago, before there were any books or storytellers, or any humans at all, there was no wind. Then one day . . .*

Read your legend to someone else and use different voices and movements to tell your story, like a traditional storyteller would do.

Exercise 5: Record a Day in the Life of the Wind

Pretend *you* are the wind. Write a journal about a day in your life. You might make it funny or serious or both. Begin writing about this day as if it is an hour before sunrise. Where are you? Are you asleep or have you been traveling in disguise all night?

Write down your activities all through the day. Where do you go? What and who do you see? What do you do? Still pretending to be the wind, allow yourself to talk to the trees, the mountains, the ocean, or the people you meet. Record these encounters. Do you ever take a rest? Do you become angry, sad, or happy? What happens if you do?

Continue your journal into the evening of your day and through the night, finally ending 24 hours after you started.

Read your journal to someone else using sound effects, different voices, and body movements to make your story dramatic.

Take your imagination with you the next time you're outside on a windy day. See how you can experience the wind from a different point of view.

4

A Windmiller's Life

A windmiller's life was hard but never boring. Wind-millers went to work when the wind began to blow—pumping, grinding, or sawing. During heavy weather a miller worked for days without stopping. Like a ship's captain, he remained at his post until the storm cleared, making sure his mill made it through safely. Some mills had a shaving bench where a barber shaved the miller when he was too busy to visit the barbershop.

In the late 1500s Dutch millers had to pay a fine to the village council if they worked on Sunday. However, some of them preferred to pay the fine rather than lose a good wind. A minister once scolded a miller for working on the Lord's day. The miller replied, "If the Lord is good enough to send me wind on a Sunday, I'm going to use it!"

At Home in a Windmill

A miller and his family often lived next door to a grist mill. They might even live inside a drainage windmill that regulated water in the canals. Two doors stood on opposite sides of the mill so that when the sails were blocking one door, the family could leave the mill by the other. The living room and kitchen were on the bottom floor with bedrooms up above. The miller's children swam and fished in the canals outside.

Drainage mills, often located far from town and near the dikes, also served as inns for passing travelers. The miller's family was happy to have the company, and the visitor could fall asleep to the whoosh of giant windmill sails, creaking wooden gears, and splashing water.

What did windmillers look like? One old joke claimed that windmillers were short, strong, and agile—short because while others were growing, millers were busy working; strong from the heavy sacks they carried on their backs; and agile from running up and down stairs all day long to keep the windmill going.

Stormy Weather Woes

The wind often blew on sunny days, but it always blew on stormy ones. Windmillers had to go outside in all weather to turn the mill or adjust the sails. First, they rotated the **turn wheel** in the back of the mill until two sails were vertical. Then they fastened the turn wheel, put on the brake, and ran to the front of the mill. Next, they climbed about 20 feet up the wooden sail, untied the ropes that held the cloth, unfurled it, climbed down, and tied it at the bottom of the sails. Finally they ran around to the back of the mill, unfastened the turn wheel, and rotated the sails 90 degrees. They repeated this operation four times until all the cloth sails were spread.

When the wind blew too hard, millers went outside again and **reefed** each sail. This meant rolling up the sail partway so that some wind would blow through the sail and turn it more slowly. Millers often had to adjust the reef points

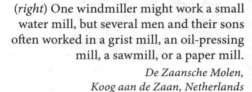

(*right*) One windmiller might work a small water mill, but several men and their sons often worked in a grist mill, an oil-pressing mill, a sawmill, or a paper mill.
De Zaansche Molen,
Koog aan de Zaan, Netherlands

(*below*) This drainage mill housed a windmiller's family as well as the machinery to drain water from the canals. The windmiller's wife even hung curtains in the window.
Seaver Center for Western History Research, Los Angeles County Museum of Natural History

several times during a storm—each time stopping and starting the mill and working on one sail at a time. In winter the sails froze as hard as boards, and so did the miller's fingers and toes.

Hazards in the Mill

Millers faced many dangers. In grist mills, millstones had to be covered with grain while the sails turned. If the grain ran out, the stones ground against each other and created sparks—a real fire hazard. Countless wooden mills burned to the ground even during rainstorms.

Millers sometimes sported with danger. During a storm they often kept their sails flying past the limits of safety, as each miller tried to prove

(*left*) Dutch families ate bread with every meal, and even the children knew how windmills helped bring fresh bread to their table. An old English nursery rhyme tells the story: "Blow, wind, blow! And go, mill, go! / That the miller may grind his corn, / That the baker may take it, / And into bread make it, / And send us some hot in the morn."
Nursery Rhymes of England by James Orchard Halliwell, Seaver Center for Western History Research, Los Angeles County Museum of Natural History

(*right*) In wintertime the Dutch loved to skate on the frozen canals, as shown in this photograph from 1911. They held long races that went through many villages. Skaters stopped at each windmill along the way to get their race card stamped. Those who completed the race before sunset received a medal. Today such races are rarely held since, because of climate change, canal ice seldom freezes thick enough.
De Zaansche Molen, Koog aan de Zaan, Netherlands

31

himself braver than the rest. But as soon as one miller removed his sails, the other millers followed suit.

Lightning bolts, attracted to tall objects in the landscape, struck many a windmill. If lightning didn't burn the mill, its heat could fuse the metal parts in the mill's machinery, and its force could fling about everything inside the mill, including the miller.

Countless millers were injured or killed by their mills. Limbs were broken and bodies were crushed by the sails or heavy gears that broke or ran out of control. A sudden **squall** could dislodge the cap of a tower mill. The wind blowing against a postmill could topple the entire structure.

Narrow escapes were common, too. An English millwright named John Bryant was repairing a sail one day when the wind began to blow and the sails began to turn. The owner of the mill had neglected to fasten the brake and had retired to a local pub. To save himself from a nasty fall, Bryant jammed his hands and one leg into a wooden arm of the windmill when it began to revolve. A passerby saw what was happening and ran to put on the brake. However, when the mill came to a stop, Bryant was hanging upside down. Following Bryant's breathless instructions, the passerby helped Bryant get his feet back on the ground. But his hands were so sore that he had to attach the reins of his horse to his elbows for the carriage ride home.

Health Hazards

Accidents weren't the only hazards of milling. The constant pounding of heavy wooden hammers against the oil press made miller's deafness common among oil millers.

A paint miller, who ground wood for paint dyes, wore a wet sponge over his mouth and nose and had to drink huge quantities of milk to keep from being poisoned by the wood dust. A miller breathed and swallowed dust all day long, but milk helped "bind" the dust and remove it from his stomach before it was absorbed into his bloodstream.

When the Wind Died Down

When the wind stopped blowing, windmillers still kept busy. Millwrights supervised major repairs, but the miller did many small repairs

These windmillers are grinding pigments for paint in this restored mill. The huge grindstones and giant beams and gears, along with flammable materials and toxic chemicals, made windmills a hazardous place to work. *De Zaansche Molen, Koog aan de Zaan, Netherlands*

himself. He lubricated all the gears, including hundreds of wooden teeth, using beeswax, three or four times a year. If he had any iron or steel parts he greased those with pig's fat—the older the better. Lumps of fat were hung from the rafters for 20 years or more before the miller used them to grease the metal.

A grain miller could tell if his millstones were in good condition by the color of the flour and the condition of the bran. He took a pinch of flour and rubbed it between his finger and his thumb. If it was fine enough, he gave it to the customer. If not, he hoisted it to the top of the mill and ground it again. This was the miller's "rule of thumb" that everyone trusted. Today we still use the expression "rule of thumb" to mean a certain way of doing things that is not precisely measured or explained but that seems to work well enough for people to accept. If the flour looked a bit coarse or burned, the miller "put his nose to the grindstone" and inspected the stones. Today we use this expression when we describe someone who concentrates and works hard.

Dressing Millstones

Millstones had to be "dressed" or sharpened just right to grind the grain evenly. **Cracks** were lines cut across the millstones. When the edges of the cracks were no longer sharp, it was time to dress the millstones—usually every week or two. **Stone dressers** roamed the countryside looking for work, but some millers preferred to do the job themselves. Like many of the miller's tasks, it was an exacting one.

A grinding stone was very hard, and as a stone dresser chipped away at it, slivers of steel flew off the dressing tool and embedded themselves in the back of his hand. When an unknown stone dresser arrived in town looking for work, a miller would ask him to "show his metal." The stranger held out the back of his hand and the more blackened bits of metal the miller saw there, he assumed, the longer the man had worked at his trade. Today the expression "show your metal" means almost the same thing—show me what you've done.

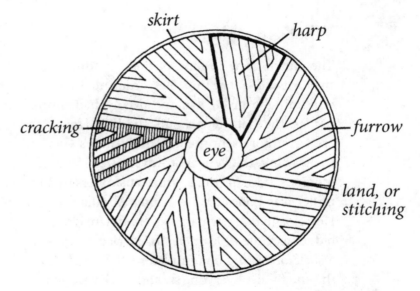

Millstones were cut or "dressed" with iron chisels so that they would grind smoothly and evenly. "Furrows" are the raised areas of the stone; "lands" are the spaces in between. "Cracking" are the shallow lines carved into the furrows. Some millstones were made of one large piece of stone that might weigh more than two tons. Others had 8 to 28 smaller stones cemented together and bound with an iron hoop or "skirt." This millstone had 10 pieces shaped like harps.
John Freeman, Perth and Kinross Council, Scotland

Windmill Weatherman

The windmiller often became the village weatherman. He could tell better than anyone else when the weather would change, where the storms would break, and of course, how much the wind would blow.

Grain mills became popular gathering places in the village. Housewives visited often to buy their flour. What better place to hear the latest gossip and add a story or two of their own? The fresh tales from the windmiller were often passed around the supper table quicker than the fresh bread made from the flour he ground that day.

What's in a Name?

The Dutch grew so fond of their windmills that they passed a law in 1693 ordering that each windmill be given a name. Many had animal names: the Cat, the Seagull, the Iron Hog. Others were more sentimental: the Prince's Garden, the Darling, the Wheel of Adventure. Some were religious, perhaps to convince customers that the miller was honest: Wise Young Abraham or the Hero Joshua. A few names were downright morbid. One, called Bleak Death, carried a sign with a skeleton sitting on a millstone that read, "I am the end of life. Everyone should work hard to prepare for me, because I work all the time."

Not every miller felt so grim about his work. Two mills, called De Juffer (the Young Lady) and De Jonker (the Squire), stood side by side on the Zaan River. It wasn't long before the nearby millers made up the following rhyme:

De Jufler en De Jonker
Zoenen elkaar in 't donker.

In English it goes like this:

The Young Lady and the Squire
Kissed each other in the dark.

One paper mill carried the following sign:

Rags make paper,
Paper makes money,
Money makes banks,
Banks make loans,
Loans make beggars,
Beggars make rags.

(Source: Molenmuseum,
Koog A/D Zaan, Netherlands)

A sense of humor sometimes made a miller's job a little easier. People also invented many tales that poked fun at millers. One was found in old manuscripts and printed books all over Europe:

It had been a long day and the miller's horse was tired from carrying a heavy sack of grain.
"Good boy," said the miller. "You've done a hard day's work. I'll take that heavy sack off your back and carry it myself."
So the miller lifted the sack off the horse and threw it across his shoulders. After they had gone a few steps, the miller noticed the horse walking more quickly.

"Since you're not carrying the load of grain, then you can carry me," he said to the horse. So the miller put himself and the sack on the poor horse's back and made his way home.

"Talking" Windmills

Millers used windmills to send messages to their neighbors. When their workday was over, windmillers set their sails to form a cross. Everyone in town knew that this meant the miller had finished work for the day and would start again tomorrow morning. If the sails were set in an X, it meant the mill was closed for the weekend or the miller was on vacation. Villagers postponed a visit to the mill when the sails were set in a cross and the top sail was covered with cloth. This meant the miller was making repairs.

When his children got married or a baby was born, a miller might weave streamers through the sails and fly flags from the top sail. Other millers decorated their sails too, and turned them to face their lucky neighbor. When the top sail pointed to eleven o'clock, this meant that the miller was mourning a death in the family.

Some British millers near the seacoast hid smuggled goods in their windmills. Using sail signals, millers told smugglers to keep away when customs agents were in the neighborhood.

Windmillers tried to protect people from danger by using sail signals. During the Protestant Reformation in the 1600s, Dutch Catholics were not allowed to practice their faith. Some

(*above*) An illustration of the story of the miller and his horse.
Library of Congress, Prints and Photographs USZ62-26693

(*left*) Windmillers still decorate windmills at holiday time. The red, white, and blue striped flag of the Netherlands flies from the top of the windmill sails.
Netherlands Board of Tourism

35

windmillers positioned their sails to indicate where secret Catholic services were held each week. In 1939, when the German Army conquered the Netherlands in five days, windmills throughout the land carried the message of the invasion using the position of their sails. This gave people a few precious hours to escape or hide their valuable possessions.

During World War II members of the Dutch Resistance, who fought the Germans in secret, sent windmill signals to each other. For example, when British and American pilots were shot down over the Netherlands, local windmillers signaled the airmen's location and many pilots were rescued.

Windmills began as machines to ease the hard labor of peasants. As time passed windmills and millers acquired a unique language, art, and folklore. For nearly 700 years windmills were the most powerful machines in Europe, well integrated into many communities. Then, during the 1800s, steam engines took their place and the old windmills began to disappear from the landscape.

Alphonse Daudet's Windmill in Fontvieille is a painting by Vincent van Gogh (1852–1890), who grew up in the Dutch countryside. After moving to France he painted the windmills that reminded him of his homeland.

*Amsterdam, Van Gogh Museum
(Vincent Van Gogh Foundation)*

CREATE LANDSCAPE ART

The seventeenth century is referred to as the golden age of Dutch windmills and Dutch landscape painting. Artists painted the land around them, and this land included windmills. Sometimes artists focused on the windmill alone (see Rembrandt's engraving on page 2). Other times painters gave a wide view of the land (see Ruisdael's painting on page 4 and van Gogh's painting on page 36). Landscape painting crossed the Atlantic when Europeans settled in the New World. North America, with its vast mountains, rivers, deserts, and seacoast attracted many landscape painters in the 1800s. Today many artists still love to paint the world they see around them.

Goal: Observe and draw the world around you—draw your landscape.

Materials

* Pad of drawing paper
* Pencil
* Eraser
* Watercolor paints, colored pencils, or crayons

Directions

Look closely at the landscape where you live. Are there hills or mountains, plains or seacoast, woods or desert? If you live in a town or city, do you have old or new buildings, high apartment houses or single-family homes, factories or office buildings? What sort of landscape lies outside the city?

Look at your landscape with an artist's eye. What would you like to draw—the view from the top of a hill or a shady spot in the park? Perhaps you prefer a busy street with shops, people, and cars going by. These views are called cityscapes.

Choose a location where you can sit for a while and make several drawings. Pencils or crayons are easiest to use when you're outside. When you're finished with a drawing, examine it. Does one thing in your scene stand out—a tree, a grain elevator, a tall building? You can draw this object up close so it appears large in the drawing or you can draw it from far away so that it blends into the landscape. Try drawing the same scene from different points of view or choose different details to emphasize.

Many artists use such drawings as guides to make larger paintings. Try making a painting from one of your sketches. Draw and paint your landscape in different seasons. Which season do you prefer to draw?

Bonus step: Visit a local art museum or library and look for examples of landscapes painted by other artists. Did they see the landscape the same way you did? Look for ideas you can use to make more landscape art.

BAKE WHOLE WHEAT ROLLS

Traditional meals in the Netherlands always included bread. Polders (the reclaimed lands) were ideal for dairy farming, so the Dutch ate a lot of butter and cheese, too. And they still do! Making bread takes some time (about four hours), but it's not a lot of work—most of the time the bread is rising on its own. Be sure to use a timer. If the bread rises too long or not long enough, it won't be light and tasty.

Goal: Bake and enjoy a Dutch treat.

Adult supervision required

Ingredients

* 1 package dry yeast
* ½ cup warm water
* 2 cups unbleached flour
* 3 cups whole wheat flour
* 2 tablespoons honey
* 1½ cups warm water
* 4 tablespoons vegetable oil
* 1 teaspoon salt
* 1 cup whole wheat flour (for kneading)
* Butter
* Dutch cheese—Edam or Gouda cheese, available in your supermarket (Note: Gouda is pronounced "HOW-da" in Dutch.)
* Apple cider

Utensils

* 1 medium-sized mixing bowl
* 1 large mixing bowl
* Measuring cup
* Measuring spoons
* Wire whisk or wooden spoon
* 2 clean dish towels

Directions

Stir dry yeast into ½ cup warm water. The water should be warm, but not hot (about 90°F). Let this sit for about 10 minutes, until a foam appears on top.

In the medium-sized mixing bowl, combine 2 cups unbleached flour with 3 cups whole wheat flour.

In the large bowl, mix honey, 1½ cups warm water, and oil. Stir until honey is dissolved.

Add yeast mixture and 2 cups of the flour mixture to the liquid mixture. Stir with a spoon or a whisk until all the lumps are gone. This will be a soupy mixture similar to pancake batter. It's called a sponge.

Use a clean dish towel to cover the bowl containing your sponge and set it in a warm place (between 70°F and 80°F). Don't set in a drafty place. If your stove has pilot lights you can put it on top of an (unlighted) burner or in the unheated oven. Let it rise until it doubles in size—about 1 hour.

Add the salt to the rest of the flour. Add this mixture to the bowl containing the sponge. Stir until thoroughly mixed. You will have a sticky dough.

Sprinkle some whole wheat flour on a clean, dry counter and on your hands. Remove the sticky sponge dough from the bowl. Knead the dough by pressing it into the counter with the heels of your hands. Do this two or three times, then fold the dough in half and add more flour to the counter and your hands. Continue to knead for about 10 minutes, until the dough is smooth, elastic, and no longer sticky. (Note: You may use less than 1 cup of flour while kneading, or you may use a bit more.)

Return the dough to a clean, large mixing bowl, cover with a towel, and set in a warm place to rise until it doubles in size, 45 to 60 minutes.

When the dough has risen, punch it down to its original size and shape into small balls about 2 inches in diameter. Place these spread out in two well-oiled round cake pans. (They will expand and join together while they cook.) Cover the rolls with dish towels and let rise another 20 minutes.

Preheat oven to 375°F. Bake rolls for 20 to 25 minutes or until golden brown. Makes 24 rolls.

Eat your Dutch rolls hot from the oven. Spread them with butter or Dutch cheese or both. Apple cider is a favorite drink in Holland. Try it with your Dutch treat!

5

All-American Windmills

"*Goede morgen, Mevrouw Pietersen*," said the miller to the plump Dutch housewife entering his windmill.

"*Ook goede morgen, Mijnheer de Molenaar*," she said to the miller as a screech filled the air.

"*The sawmill received a shipment of timber this morning*," explained the miller. "*That's the first log going through the saw. This strong wind may last for two or three days, and you can be sure the sawyers will keep us awake tonight.*"

Where was this scene? It could have been in many Dutch towns in the 1600s, but it was actually thousands of miles away in New York City. Dutch merchants bought the island of Manhattan and built a town called New Amsterdam in the 1620s. They didn't keep it for long. In 1664 the English took over and changed the name to New York. By that time the Dutch had built a string of windmills from the Battery to Park Row. When the government changed hands, most Dutch settlers stayed in New York, and so did their windmills.

Windmills were so important in colonial New York City that the official city seal, designed in 1784, shows four windmill sails and two barrels of flour. This is still used today. *New York City Department of General Services*

The Dutch bought the island of Manhattan from the Native North Americans in 1626 and called their settlement New Amsterdam. Windmills were a common sight along the Hudson River. When the English took over in 1664 the windmills remained. *Seaver Center for Western History, Research, Los Angeles County Museum of Natural History*

Dutch millwrights also built windmills in Breukelen (Brooklyn) and up the Hudson River Valley. English millwrights built smock mills and postmills from Cape Cod to Long Island and south to the Carolinas. Windmillers worked their windmills just as they had done in Europe.

Inventors Take Up the Challenge

Until 1850 the American West belonged to Native North Americans who followed herds of bison and made camp near rivers and streams. When white settlers first looked west, across the Mississippi River, they saw land that was too dry to farm or graze cattle on. They even nicknamed it the Great American Desert. There didn't seem to be enough water to make this region habitable.

In 1860 a Texan wrote to *Scientific American* magazine, "The great want of Texas is water. . . . There is a million dollars lying waiting for the first man who will bring us a windmill—strong, durable, and controllable." Dozens of inventors took up the challenge.

In Connecticut a mechanic named Daniel Halladay claimed he could invent a windmill that would automatically stop working in high winds. But he couldn't imagine "a single man in the world who would want one." John Burnham knew otherwise. He fixed windmills that broke because farmers were too busy to take down the sails when the wind blew too hard. He persuaded Halladay to put his Yankee ingenuity to work.

Halladay invented a small windmill on a wooden tower. Gone was the smock that held it up and gone were the four huge sails that caught the wind. Instead, Halladay arranged a dozen or more thin wooden slats around a hub. When the wind blew too hard, the fan of wind vanes swung so the wind blew through them and saved the mill from blowing apart.

Halladay didn't have much success selling his windmills in New England, so he and Burnham moved to Chicago—the Windy City. They set up a windmill factory in nearby Batavia, Illinois.

Reverend Leonard R. Wheeler, who ran a Christian mission for Native North Americans in Wisconsin, also invented a new windmill. Like Halladay, he used a simple tower and thin wooden wind vanes, but his machine had a small side wind vane that turned the whole wheel sideways in a strong wind. He called it the **Eclipse windmill**.

The new **North American windmills** were less powerful than the old European models, but they could do the job that was needed—pumping water. Strictly speaking, they weren't windmills because they didn't mill (grind); they pumped. But everyone called them windmills nonetheless.

Windmills on the Railroad

After the Civil War ended in 1865, people rushed to settle the West. Railroads snaked their way across the Great Plains. The coal-burning steam locomotives needed about 2,000 gallons of water every 20 miles. Railroad workers collected water from nearby streams, or filled railroad cars with water, or relied on windmills.

The railroad trade was a prize for any windmill company. Union Pacific bought 70 giant

(*top*) This early windmill was built on top of a hill in Newport, Rhode Island, to catch the breeze that blows off the ocean. Rhode Island, Cape Cod, and Long Island have many old windmills restored to working order.

Library of Congress, Prints and Photographs, USZ62-32567

(*left*) Nineteenth-century factory-made windmills were small, easily assembled, and relatively cheap. They used interchangeable parts, ran automatically, and needed little care. Many American farms and ranches were so large that a rancher might not visit his windmill for months.

Original advertising cards, Batavia Historical Society, Batavia, Illinois

Halladay windmills for the first transcontinental railroad. Smaller Eclipse mills watered the engines of the Burlington, Northwestern, Illinois Central, and Atchison, Topeka, and Santa Fe railroads. Large windmills could lift water 150 feet and began to turn at wind speeds as low as six mph.

Windmills on the Farm

Farmers needed water for their houses and vegetable gardens, and ranchers had to fill livestock watering troughs. Pioneers bought windmills and towers from traveling salesmen or from mail-order catalogs. Most companies painted the company's name on the **rudder**, but Sears Roebuck offered to paint the owner's name free of charge.

Many farmers had no money to spare, so they built their own windmills. In 1897 Professor Erwin Barbour of the University of Nebraska sent students on a field trip to photograph these homemade windmills. They left Lincoln, Nebraska, with horses, camping wagons, and cameras and traveled to Denver, Colorado. The students found wind machines made from bits of broken machinery, scrap iron, and wood. These mills had nicknames like Go-Devil, Ground Tumbler, Jumbo, Baby Jumbo, Merry-Go-Round, and Battle-Ax. They weren't as efficient as factory models, but that didn't seem to matter. Professor Barbour said, "they cost little, work well, and do all the work that is laid on them."

The Great Plains suffered terrible droughts that could last for years. Windmills couldn't

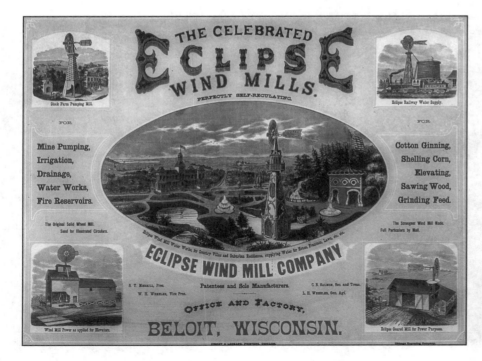

irrigate the vast fields of wheat and corn that the farmers grew as cash crops, but they could water an acre of vegetables near the farmhouse. In drought years, a windmill could mean the difference between survival and starvation.

A child in Cherry County, Nebraska, said it in poetry.

> We like it in the sandhills,
> We like it very good,
> For the wind it pumps our water,
> And the cows they chop our wood.

How did cows chop wood? They didn't really. The Western plains had few, if any, trees to chop. Instead pioneers burned buffalo or cow chips—manure that had dried in the hot prairie sun. It wasn't really wood and cows didn't chop it, but cows did provide fuel to cook the meals and heat the sod houses of early settlers. And out in the yard the wind pumped the water they needed.

Hardy Workers

Windmills performed many labor-saving tasks in the American West. They sawed wood and ran the cotton gin. They hoisted grain into tall silos. They pumped water from mine shafts and crushed ore when it came out of the ground. They ran turning lathes for carpenters and even powered a printing press in Sauk Center, Minnesota. The newspaper editor couldn't resist a joke about his windmill press. He said, "Wind is an important agent in the running of political newspapers, especially about election time, but its employment in such

Some farmers couldn't afford a factory-built windmill, so they made their own. This eight-bladed Battle-Ax windmill photographed in 1898 near Grand Island, Nebraska, cost $14 to make.
US Geological Survey Photographic Library, Barbour Collection #21

These Nebraska homesteaders from the 1880s made their sod house by hand but bought a factory-made windmill. The family probably owned little more than what we see here—a few horses, some cattle, and a windmill.
Nebraska State Historical Society

prosaic service as doing useful commercial printing is, we believe, quite exceptional."

One proud owner bragged that his Eclipse windmill "grinds all the feed for six horses and twenty-four head of cattle and hogs, shells all the corn, does all the pumping for the stock, saws all our wood, and runs a wooden-turn lathe and grindstone. It does all the churning every day, runs a washing machine, and last but not least, runs a crank pipe organ so that the girls can have a song and dance while the machine is doing their work. This may sound a little strange, but it is perfectly true."

Strange? Yes. True? Perhaps.

Gold miners in California needed salt to preserve their meat and process ore, so enterprising men built salt works in San Francisco Bay. This 1912 photograph shows how windmills pumped saltwater from one evaporation pond to another.
US Geological Survey Photographic Library, Phalen Collection #329

BAKE COLONIAL APPLE-CRANBERRY COBBLER

New England settlers brought apple cobbler from England and discovered native cranberries in North America. Cranberries alone are sour, but when mixed with apples and sugar, they form a sweet-and-sour treat. Colonial millers ground whole wheat flour, but you can mix whole wheat and white flour if you like.

Goal: Bake and enjoy a sweet New England treat.

Adult supervision required

Fruit Filling

* 4 or 5 green cooking apples
* 1 cup whole cranberry sauce, canned or fresh
* 3 tablespoons brown sugar

Topping

* 1 cup whole wheat pastry flour or ½ cup white flour and ½ cup whole wheat flour
* 1 tablespoon white sugar
* 1 teaspoon baking powder
* ½ teaspoon baking soda
* ¼ teaspoon salt
* 3 tablespoons butter
* ½ cup milk
* Ice cream, yogurt, or milk

Utensils

* Knife
* Measuring cup
* Casserole dish, 9 by 9 inches
* Large mixing bowl
* Measuring spoons
* Pastry cutter or fork
* Large spoon

Directions

Preheat oven to 350°F. Slice apples to make 4 cups. Place in lightly greased casserole dish. Add cranberry sauce and brown sugar; mix thoroughly. In bowl combine flour, white sugar, baking powder, baking soda, and salt.

Add butter. Using a pastry cutter or fork, cut up the butter until completely blended with flour mixture. Add milk and stir.

The dough will be sticky. Drop spoonfuls of the dough on top of the fruit to make your "cobbles." A fruit cobbler is meant to look like a bumpy cobblestone street, so don't make your topping modern-highway smooth. Also, don't try to cover every bit of fruit. The dough will spread out during baking. Bake for 40 minutes or so, until the crust is golden brown.

You can use your windmill-patterned pot holder to take the Colonial Apple-Cranberry Cobbler out of the oven. Eat it while it's hot, topped with ice cream, yogurt, or milk.

CREATE A WINDMILL PAPER COLLAGE

Early American settlers made almost everything they needed. Women sewed clothing for the family. They used pieces of leftover fabric and worn-out clothes to make patchwork quilts. Quilt making gave women a chance to express artistic ideas in a practical way. They took objects from daily life—like wedding rings, log cabins, and windmills—and invented quilt patterns that reminded them of those objects.

Goal: *Create a windmill pattern out of colorful paper.*

Materials

* Ruler
* 3 pieces of construction paper or gift wrap of different colors or patterns:
* Color 1, 3½ by 7 inches
* Color 2, 3½ by 3½ inches
* Color 3, 3½ by 3½ inches (this will make the windmill sails and should be brighter than the other pieces; or try a patterned paper)
* Scissors
* Sheet of heavy drawing paper or poster board, 8½ by 11 inches
* Pencil
* Glue

Directions

Fold Color 1 in half to make two 3½-inch squares. Cut on fold line. Fold these squares on the diagonal and cut along the fold. This will make four right-angle triangles.

Fold Color 2 in half to make two right-angle triangles, each right-angle side measuring 3½ inches. Cut along the fold.

Fold Color 3 in half to make two right-angle triangles, each right-angle side measuring 3½ inches. Cut along the fold.

Fold Color 2 and Color 3 triangles on the diagonal again. Cut along the fold. You will have four small right-angle triangles, each right-angle side measuring 2½ inches.

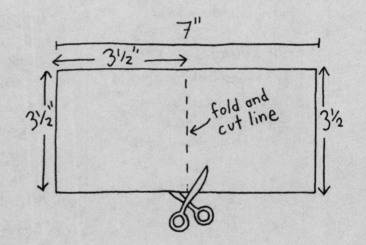

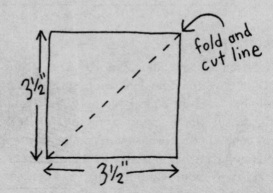

Lay all the triangles on the heavy paper, using it as a picture frame, to form a windmill pattern. Be sure the windmill sails are in the right position and facing the right direction, as shown in the illustration. Leave a border on all sides. With a pencil and ruler, lightly draw along the outside edge of your collage.

Glue each triangle in place on the picture frame. When finished, display your collage by pinning it to a bulletin board or hanging it on a wall. Can you see the windmill sails spin? You can also make a collage using pieces of fabric. Instead of using glue to secure the triangles, use a needle and thread.

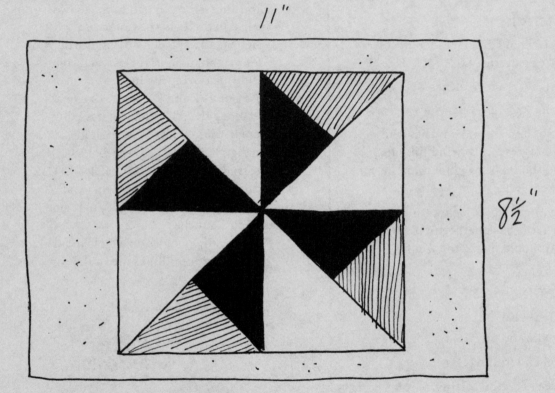

11"

8½"

SEW A WINDMILL POT HOLDER

You can sew this pot holder by hand or on a sewing machine.

Goal: Create a windmill-patterned pot holder with colorful fabric.

Adult supervision required

Materials

* 4 pieces of fabric of different colors or patterns:
* Color 1, 3½ by 7 inches
* Color 2, 3½ by 3½ inches
* Color 3A, 3½ by 3½ inches (this will represent the windmill sails and should be brighter than the other pieces; or try a pattern)
* Color 3B, 7 by 7 inches (this will form the back of the pot holder and should match the windmill sails)
* Scissors
* Straight pins
* Needle and thread
* Iron and ironing board
* Piece of cotton batting, 6 by 6 inches
* Plastic ring, ½ inch in diameter

Directions

Fold and cut Color 1 in half to make two 3½-inch squares. Fold the Color 1 squares on the diagonal and cut along the fold. You will have four right-angle triangles, each right-angle side measuring 3½ inches.

Fold Colors 2 and 3A on the diagonal and cut along the fold. You will have four right-angle triangles, each right-angle side measuring 3½ inches. Fold the Colors 2 and 3A triangles on the diagonal again. Cut along the fold. You will have eight small right-angle triangles, each right angle side measuring 2½ inches.

Lay all your triangles on a table to form the windmill pattern illustrated on the next page. Be sure your windmill sails are in the right position.

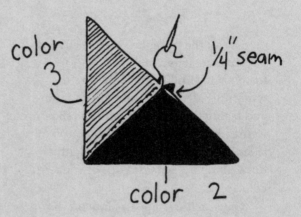

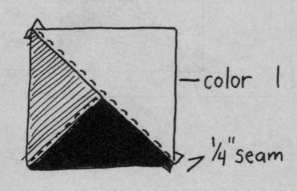

Pin the smaller triangles together (Colors 2 and 3A), with the right sides of the fabric together. You'll make four right-angle triangles, each right angle side measuring 3½ inches. Sew these triangles together with a ¼-inch seam. Iron the seams flat.

Form the windmill pattern again. Pin the sewn triangle to a Color 1 triangle to form a square. Pin the right sides of the fabric together. Repeat until you have four squares.

Sew the squares together with a ¼-inch seam. Iron the seams flat.

Form the windmill pattern again with your four squares. Pin your four squares together, right sides of the fabric together, to form one large square, approximately 6½ inches on each side. You'll have one 6½-inch vertical seam and one 6½-inch horizontal seam. Sew the seams with a ¼-inch seam. Again, iron the seams flat.

Lay the windmill pattern square on the 7-by-7-inch Color 3B square, with right sides of the fabric together. Pin three sides of the square. Sew the three sides with a ¼-inch seam.

Turn the pot holder right side out. Insert the square of batting.

Fold the two open edges of the square to make a seam. Pin the edges and then sew them together. Sew the plastic ring to one corner of the pot holder so you can hang it up for all to see.

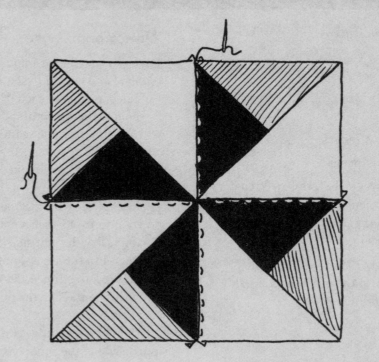

MAKE A WINDMILL PILLOW COVER

Make four windmill squares to cover a small cushion or pillow. Organize an old-fashioned quilting bee—invite some friends to help and you'll be surprised how fast the work gets done.

Goal: Create a windmill pattern on a decorative pillow.

Adult supervision required

Materials

✳ 4 pieces of fabric of different colors or patterns:

✳ Color 1, 7 by 14 inches

✳ Color 2, 7 by 7 inches

✳ Color 3A, 7 by 7 inches (this will represent the windmill sails and should be brighter than the other pieces; or try a patterned piece)

✳ Color 3B, 13 by 13 inches (this will form the back of the pillow and should match the windmill sails)

✳ Scissors

✳ Straight pins

✳ Needle and thread

✳ Iron and ironing board

✳ 1 pillow or uncovered cushion, 12 by 12 inches

✳ 7 to 9 medium-sized snaps

Directions

Fold and cut Color 1 in quarters to make four pieces, each 3½ by 7 inches.

Fold and cut colors 2 and 3A into quarters to make four pieces, each 3½ inches square. Select one piece each of colors 1, 2, and 3A and set the others aside.

Follow the windmill pot holder directions through the seventh paragraph (ending with "Again, iron the seams flat"). Make three more windmill pattern squares (four in all).

Pin the four squares together, right sides of the fabric together. You will have one 12-inch vertical seam and one 12-inch horizontal seam. Sew together with a ¼-inch seam. Iron the seams flat.

Lay the big windmill pattern on your 13-by-13-inch square (Color 3B), with right sides together. Pin three sides of the square. Sew the three sides with a ¼-inch seam. Turn the pillow cover right side out.

Hem both raw edges on the fourth side of the square as follows. Fold the raw edge ¼ inch. Then fold another ¼ inch to make a smooth edge. Sew seam. Repeat with second raw edge. This side of the pillow cover will still be open.

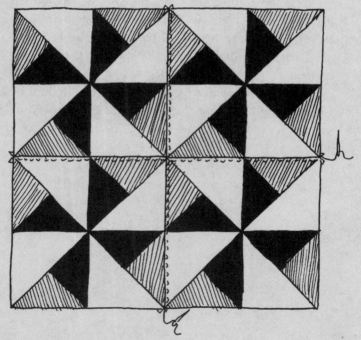

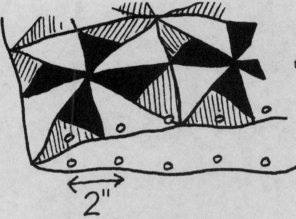

Sew snaps every 2 inches along both edges of the open end of the pillow cover. Be sure the two parts of the snaps line up with each other before sewing, as shown.

Insert the pillow into the pillow cover and put it in a prominent place for all to see.

6
Inventors and Cowboys Work the Wind

In the early 1880s Thomas O. Perry, an engineer at Daniel Halladay's United States Wind Engine and Pump Company, conducted the first scientific studies of windmills. Perry invented a wind tunnel and steam-powered sweep (wind machine) that spun windmills at controlled speeds. He also invented instruments to measure wind speeds, temperature, and barometric pressure.

Perry completed more than 5,000 windmill experiments. He tested many different models in different wind and climate conditions. He tinkered with the wind vanes. He tried different materials. He attached wind vanes at different angles. Some people laughed at Perry's scientific principles and his **mathematical windmill**, but that didn't stop him.

He wanted to design a windmill that would work in light as well as heavy winds. He replaced flat wooden blades with concave steel blades set at a new angle to produce low wind resistance and high strength. Perry worked for more than a year in a locked test chamber with guards at the door. He claimed that he locked it to control his experiments. Some people said he was afraid of spies. When he was satisfied with his results, he presented his new windmill to the board of directors at Halladay's company. They rejected it. Halladay's company, which had been so revolutionary back in the 1850s, had grown conservative in middle age. So Perry took his design elsewhere. He met inventor-businessman La Verne Noyes, and together they started the Aermotor Company to manufacture Perry's mathematical windmill.

Wood Versus Steel

Early windmills were made of wood with a few metal fittings. Metal wind vanes were often weak and always hard to repair. They also rusted easily.

Makers of wooden mills boasted that "All good wood mills will outlast two steel mills of anybody's make."

The **Aermotor windmill**'s new design converted many owners—but not all—from wooden to steel windmills. But disagreements didn't stop there. Metal windmill owners argued about the best way to prevent rust on the steel mills. Some favored paint; others favored galvanizing. This meant dipping the metal parts into molten zinc—an element that resists rust. In the galvanizers' camp, there were groups that believed in galvanizing windmill parts before they were put together. Others insisted on galvanizing

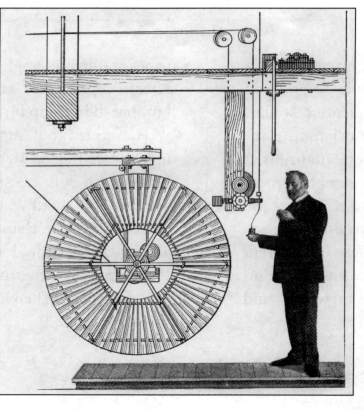

(left) In the 1880s Thomas O. Perry performed more than 5,000 experiments on windmills. This fanciful collage shows him with part of his scientific apparatus.
US Geological Survey Water Supply Paper, 1899

(right) Perry's windmill used concave steel blades set at a precise angle to spin faster and last longer. But some ranchers liked their old flat, wooden-bladed windmills and saw no reason to adopt the new "mathematical" model.
Panhandle-Plains Historical Museum, Research Center, Canyon, Texas

afterward. Western ranchers and farmers were an outspoken lot. They never agreed on one best windmill.

A Matter of Pride

By 1889 there were 77 windmill companies in the United States, and intense rivalries sprang up. It was not just about who sold more windmills; it was also about loyalty. Windmill factory workers took pride in their work.

In 1893 the World's Columbian Exposition opened in Chicago, and 21 million people wandered through 200 buildings to see the most advanced technology from around the world. A person would have to walk 150 miles just to see all of the latest inventions in electricity, machinery, and many other fields. Giant steam engines, Thomas Edison's talking films, and the world's largest Ferris wheel drew the biggest crowds.

Tucked in back of the agriculture hall dozens of old familiar windmills, from 15 different companies, blew in the breeze. A smock mill, imported from the Netherlands, ground cocoa while Dutch girls in traditional costume served hot chocolate. Windmills from North America ground and chopped cattle feed, shelled corn, pumped water, and sawed lumber.

The owners of the Aermotor Company saw a chance to attract more attention by erecting a windmill behind the livestock pavilion to cut and grind feed for the animals. Other companies protested. They wanted extra publicity, too. Harsh words flew back and forth. One evening, while the Aermotor crew was at dinner, a group of men

stole into the livestock area and pulled down the windmill. Tempers grew even hotter and fights broke out. Aermotor rebuilt it and offered to pay shipping charges to bring other windmills to the livestock pavilion, but by then the exposition was nearly over. In the end, only the Aermotor windmill rose above the pigpens.

North American Windmills Abroad

North American windmills traveled far afield. In 1906 a reporter named Frank O. Medlock wrote, "From the mining camps of Alaska, where it pumps water to wash out the gold, to the very heart

One visitor described the Chicago Columbian Exposition windmills this way: "Numerous tall towers, like the masts of ships grouped closely in harbor with colors flying, surmounted by wind wheels of various forms and sizes whirling, in the bright sunlight and throwing off sparkling rays of many colors that afford from the distance a unique, lively, and brilliant spectacle."
Illinois State Historical Library

of Africa, where it grinds grain for the natives, and so on clear around the globe, the windmill is faithfully doing its work. Windmills are exported from the United States to South America, South Africa, Australia, and other agricultural and grazing countries. But the United States is the greatest country in the world for windmills."

America exports these windmills today. The old-style North American windmill is still the cheapest way to pump water in dry, windy lands.

Windmillers of the Wild West

As windmills sprang up across the Great Plains, so did a new character—the North American windmiller. His European cousin would never have recognized him. In Europe, windmills passed from father to son, and a family of millers often lived in the same town for centuries. They never went far from home, worked day and night at the mill, and knew everyone in town.

American windmillers were different in almost every respect. They were loners, traveling from ranch to ranch in horse-drawn wagons—and later on, cars—each with a tool chest and perhaps a dog to keep him company. Many were former cowboys, but they didn't sleep in the bunkhouse with the other hired hands. Nighttime found them camping in their wagons or under the stars.

(left) Windmillers camped out as they traveled from ranch to ranch. A cook who could make good beans and coffee over a campfire was welcome on any crew.
Panhandle-Plains Historical Museum, Research Center, Canyon, Texas

(right) High on the towers, millers oiled the windmills and replaced broken parts. They also repaired the pumps that lifted the water from deep underground.
Panhandle-Plains Historical Museum, Research Center, Canyon, Texas

Though the rancher hardly knew him, a wind-miller was as important to him as the traveling doctor or the veterinarian. When a new windmill arrived from the factory, a windmiller helped the rancher put it together. He also checked, greased, and repaired old mills and water pumps. The job could be dangerous, for a strong prairie wind could blow a man off a hundred-foot tower.

All Around the Windmill Tower

Windmillers weren't the only ones to climb the windmill towers. Boys and girls often sneaked up to take a look at the finest view in the country. For example, one boy rigged up an airborne trolley by stringing a wire from the windmill tower to the house. Another group of children were spanked for climbing a windmill tower. These adventurous kids were stopped only when their father sawed off the ladder about eight feet up.

Many grown-ups feared these heights. The huge XIT Ranch in Texas, spread over three million acres, had more than 500 windmills. Ranch hands oiled the windmills when they needed it. But some wives offered free cooking and laundry to anyone who would take their husbands' turn at oiling the windmill. When self-oiling windmills were invented, both cowboys and their wives breathed easier.

Windmill towers proved to be useful in other ways. Farmers hung lanterns from the towers to serve as beacons for travelers. Cowboys climbed to the tops of towers to look for their cattle. Ministers sometimes baptized Christians at the

As farmers became more prosperous, they moved from cramped sod houses to comfortable farmhouses. But rich or poor, they all needed a windmill to work the farm.
Illinois State Historical Library

windmill's water tank, and more than one outlaw was hanged from a windmill tower.

As the West grew more civilized, folks used windmills to pump water through pipes of their indoor plumbing—a sink in the kitchen and a toilet and bathtub in the bathroom. They would have no more outhouses and no more washtubs in the kitchen.

Six million windmills worked in the West during their heyday, from 1880 to 1935. "The prairie land is fairly alive with them," said the *Kansas City Star* in 1904. "The windmill has taken the place of the old town pump, and no Western town is complete in its public comforts without a mill supplying water to man and beast by the energy of the wind."

Historical societies and private collectors have restored some of the old North American windmills. Riverwalk in Batavia, Illinois, shown here, has a fine display. The walk passes factory buildings of the US Wind Engine and Pump Company that manufactured windmills in Batavia from the mid-1880s to the 1940s.
Courtesy of the Batavia Depot Museum

PRAIRIE COOKIN' CORN DODGERS

Windmillers, cowboys, and settlers on the Great Plains ate corn bread and beans almost every day—for breakfast, lunch, or supper. Corn bread took on many names from New England to California. Folks called it jonnycake, journey cake, or hoecake. If they didn't have an oven to bake it, they cooked little cakes in a skillet and called them corn dodgers. Out on the prairie, cowboys and windmillers cooked corn dodgers over a campfire.

Goal: Cook and eat a traditional prairie cowboy dish.

Adult supervision required

Ingredients

* 1 cup coarse yellow cornmeal
* ½ teaspoon salt
* 1 tablespoon brown sugar
* 2 tablespoons vegetable oil
* 1 cup boiling water
* 1 egg
* Honey or maple syrup

Utensils

* Measuring cup
* Measuring spoons
* Large mixing bowl
* Large spoon for mixing
* Frying pan or griddle
* Spatula

Directions

Mix cornmeal, salt, and brown sugar. Add 1 tablespoon of oil and stir until blended. Add boiling water and mix thoroughly. Beat in egg. The dough will be sticky but not runny.

Preheat a frying pan or griddle with 1 tablespoon of oil. To test if it's hot enough, sprinkle a few drops of water in the pan. When the water sizzles, the pan is ready.

Turn heat to low. Drop spoonfuls of batter into the pan. Cook for about 5 minutes or until lightly browned. Turn and cook 5 minutes on the other side.

Eat your crispy corn dodgers plain or pour honey or maple syrup on top for a sweet treat.

COOK ON-THE-TRAIL BEANS

Goal: Cook and sample another prairie dish.

Adult supervision required

Ingredients

✳ 1 pound dry pinto beans

✳ 6 cups water

✳ 3 cloves garlic, minced

✳ 1 onion, finely chopped

✳ 1 teaspoon dried sage leaves

✳ 3 tablespoons oil

✳ 3 tablespoons imitation bacon bits

✳ Salt and pepper to taste

Utensils

✳ Large pot with lid

✳ Measuring cup

✳ Measuring spoons

✳ Large spoon for mixing

✳ Ladle

✳ Potato masher

Directions

Rinse the beans. Place the beans in a large pot. Add water, garlic, onion, sage leaves, and oil. Cover and let beans soak for 4 hours or overnight.

When you are ready to cook the beans, remove the lid and add imitation bacon bits, and salt and pepper to taste. Bring the mixture to a boil and then lower the heat and simmer for about 1 hour or until tender. Stir several times during cooking.

Use a ladle to dish them into a soup bowl, or mash them with a potato masher and serve on a plate. Call your friends and family to the table with the traditional "Cowboy's Gettin'-Up Holler." Windmillers, just like cowboys, traveled from one ranch to another. They probably heard this call every morning.

Cowboy's Gettin'-Up Holler

Wake up, Jacob, day's a-breakin',
Fryin' pan's on and hoecakes bakin'.
Beans are in the pan and coffee's in the pot,
Get up now and get it while it's hot.

SING A SONG OF THE AMERICAN WEST

In 1862 Congress passed the Homestead Act, which gave 160 acres of land free to unmarried adults or heads of households. In order to gain title to (ownership of) the land, homesteaders needed to build a house on their land claim and live in it for five years. People didn't need money to obtain their government claim, but they did need a strong constitution and a sense of humor. The same wind that powered the windmills to pump water also brought blizzards, dust storms, tornadoes, and prairie fires that tested their resolve.

Goal: *Learn about the hardships of early pioneers through song.*

Materials

✳ Harmonica or guitar (optional)

Directions

After supper, serenade your family or friends with this traditional folk song about pioneer life in the old West. If someone you know plays harmonica or guitar, ask him or her to accompany you—it'll lend an authentic cowboy sound to your song. (The melody and guitar chords follow.)

Starving to Death on My Government Claim

Tom White is my name, an old bachelor I am,
You'll find me out West in the country of fame,
You'll find me out West on an elegant plain,
And starving to death on my government claim.

Hurrah for Nebraska! the land of the free,
The land of the bedbug, grasshopper, and flea,
I'll sing of its praises and tell of its fame,
While starving to death on my government claim.

My house is built of natural sod,
Its walls are erected according to hod;
Its roof has no pitch but is level and plain,
I always get wet if it happens to rain.

How happy am I when I crawl into bed!
A rattlesnake hisses a tune at my head,
A gay little centipede, all without fear,
Crawls over my pillow and into my ear.

Good-bye to Nebraska where blizzards arise,
Where the sun never sinks and a flea never dies,
And the wind never ceases but always remains
Till it starves us all out on our government claims.

Farewell to Nebraska, farewell to the West,
I'll travel back East to the girl I love best,
I'll go to Kentucky and marry me a wife,
And quit corn bread and beans for the rest of my life.

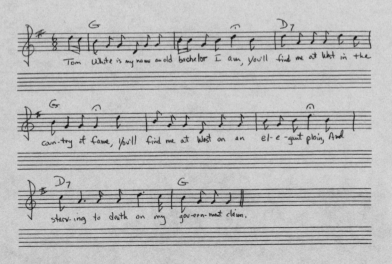

7

A New Kind of Windmill

In 1892, while windmills watered the American Great Plains, inventor Poul LaCour worked on a new sort of windmill in his native Denmark. Denmark is a flat country, and the wind there blows more than 300 days a year. Thousands of Dutch-style windmills already ground grain for flour and cattle feed, but LaCour's dream was to work the wind in a new way. In 1892 he succeeded in generating electricity with an old-fashioned Dutch windmill.

LaCour took his invention to the Danish government, and in 1903 the Danish Wind Electricity Company was formed. Within five years, 72 wind-powered generators were providing electricity to farms and villages.

In 1894 Norwegian explorer Fridtjof Nansen sailed the Arctic Ocean searching for the exact location of the North Pole. During the long, dark winter his ship was trapped in the Arctic ice. The sun did not rise above the horizon for months at a time, but Nansen's cabin glowed with electric lights thanks to LaCour's invention. Nansen had taken a small windmill and generator with him. While the great cities of New York and Paris were lit by gaslight, one small ship at the North Pole shone bright with wind-powered electric lights.

In 1892 Danish inventor Poul LaCour invented a windmill that generated electricity. He used a Dutch-style mill with large wooden sails. By 1908 Denmark had 72 windmills providing low-cost electricity to farms and villages.
Askov Hojskole, Vejen, Denmark

Windmills Bring Radio to the Farm

During the 1920s a new invention—radio—captivated American families. But radios required electricity, and most farms had none. But those farms did have windmills. Some farmers tried generating electricity with their water pumping mills, but these didn't spin fast enough. So they tried another new invention that twirled—an airplane propeller.

Farmyard tinkerers went to work using automobile generators, a storage battery, and airplane or hand-carved propellers. Many barns were crowned by these electric windmills, which ran the radio and lit a few lightbulbs besides. Homemade generators could produce 300 to 600 **watts** of electricity.

Soon more ambitious inventors improved these designs. Brothers Marcellus and Joe Jacobs, who grew up on a windy ranch in Montana, worked for years on a wind machine to generate electricity. They tried metal blades but decided wood was better. They settled on three blades for their propeller and invented a new kind of generator. Because their machine didn't "mill" or grind, they called it a wind plant. In 1932 Marcellus and Joe opened the Jacobs Wind Electric Company in Minneapolis, Minnesota, and over the years they sold tens of thousands of small generating wind plants all over the world.

The **Jacobs wind plant** could produce 400 to 500 **kilowatt-hours** per month in a windy location. This could run lights, radios, or power tools in the barn. Like the oldest windmills that eliminated the tedious work of turning millstones, these new electric windmills made life easier, too.

Explorer Rear Admiral Richard Byrd took a Jacobs wind plant to Antarctica in 1933. He installed it on top of a radio tower at the Little America base and left it there when the base was abandoned in 1935. Byrd returned 20 years later to find Little America buried in snow, all the way to the top of the radio tower—where the Jacobs wind plant blades were still spinning! When they examined the machine, they found it still generated electricity, after 20 years in the world's harshest climate!

The New Deal but Not for Windmills

In the 1930s President Franklin Roosevelt devised the New Deal to bring America out of the Great Depression. Thousands of businesses had failed following the stock market crash of 1929. From bankers to factory workers to farmers, millions of people lost their jobs.

Roosevelt wanted to put the country back to work and started massive public works projects to give people jobs and improve their lives. One of his New Deal plans was the Rural Electrification Project, which brought electric power lines to remote farms and ranches. This meant the end of most generating windmills in the American West.

In 1934, when Roosevelt's New Deal was getting started, an engineer named Palmer Putnam wanted to find a cheaper way to generate electrical power on a large scale. Most of our electricity was

Charles Brush, a wealthy inventor and manufacturer of electrical equipment, built this giant windmill in 1888. He used it to generate power for 350 electric lights in his mansion. A huge battery room in the basement held 408 battery cells—glass jars filled with chemicals that stored electricity generated by the wind. Brush's wind turbine was successful but very expensive.

Western Reserve Historical Society, Cleveland, Ohio

From 1933 to 1935 this Jacobs wind plant generated electricity for the Little America base in Antarctica. After the men left the base in 1935, the Jacobs generator kept spinning, until Admiral Byrd returned 20 years later to find that it still worked!

Jacobs Wind Electric Company

The Smith-Putnam wind turbine, with 80-foot blades, was a bold experiment back in the 1940s. It generated electricity on a mountain in Vermont for 18 months.
NREL/DOE

find it, when you find it—and this fuel is free. So Putnam put together a team of experts in electricity, aerodynamics, engineering, and weather to build the biggest windmill ever. They called it the **Smith-Putnam wind turbine**, and they installed it on a hill called Grandpa's Knob near Rutland, Vermont, in 1941.

The Smith-Putnam turbine weighed 250 tons and sat atop a 110-foot tower. The two blades measured 175 feet in diameter. For 18 months the huge turbine whirled in the Vermont wind and generated electricity that fed into central power lines. Then a bearing failed in 1943 and the machine was shut down.

During this time World War II was raging in Europe and the Pacific. American industry concentrated on building planes, battleships, and weapons for the war effort. So the enormous windmill in Vermont stood idle for two years. The huge blades were locked in place, and the vibrations from the wind caused hairline cracks on the blades. The engineers knew the blades should be repaired but started the wind turbine again in 1945 before the repairs were done. Three weeks later one of the giant blades broke off and crashed to the ground.

Putnam couldn't raise the money to continue the wind power experiment. The US government decided to develop nuclear power, not knowing the dangers of radioactive contamination it carried. At the same time, oil and coal continued to provide cheap, reliable power. So the giant windmill on Grandpa's Knob faded from memory. The 1950s and 1960s were prosperous times for the United States and Europe, and people's demand

generated by burning fossil fuels. (This remains true today.) Before these fuels can be burned, they have to be mined or pumped and then refined before they are transported thousands of miles by fossil-fuel-burning ships, trains, or trucks to a destination where they can be converted into energy. All these costs increased Putnam's electricity bill.

Wind power was an intriguing alternative to Putnam. Wind can generate power where you

for electricity increased. By 1970 one historian had predicted that "the twentieth century has witnessed the final decline of the windmill."

Legend has it that Mark Twain, after seeing a death notice for himself in a local paper, remarked, "Rumors of my death have been greatly exaggerated." So it was with windmills. A few years later windmills returned with a new look, a new purpose, and more promise than ever.

Marcellus Jacobs climbed up the tower to pose with a Jacobs wind plant machine in the 1940s. He chose a calm day to do it, for his hat is still on his head!
Jacobs Wind Electric Company

MAKE AN ELECTRIC INVENTORY OF YOUR HOUSE

One hundred years ago, many people didn't have electricity in their homes. When their houses were finally wired, they installed electric lights. Other inventions came later. Today we depend on electricity for dozens of activities.

Goal: Discover all the ways you use electricity by making an electrical survey of your home.

Materials

* Notebook
* Pencil

Directions

Make a chart in your notebook like the one shown below.

HOUSEHOLD ELECTRIC INVENTORY

ROOM	ELECTRICAL EQUIPMENT	HOW OFTEN USED	IMPORTANCE
Kitchen	refrigerator	24 hours/day	necessity
	garbage disposal	3 times/day	convenience
	12 lightbulbs	6 hours/day	more important at night
	ventilator fan . . .		

Walk through each room of your house and write down everything that uses electricity. Look carefully—some items may be stored in cupboards and closets. Remember to include battery-operated watches, phones, toys, and so on. (Be sure to ask permission to inspect other people's rooms.) Don't forget the garage and the basement. What about heating and cooling systems for your house? Are they electric? Do they use electric fans or starter motors? Ask your family to help estimate how much time they use each electrical item. Some are used every day, all the time (such as a refrigerator), and others may be used only once a month (such as a popcorn popper). Mark down the answers next to each item.

During a day at home, record on another sheet of paper each time you use something electrical. Title this "My Electric Inventory." Mark down each item and how many times you use it. This includes looking at an electric watch or a clock, answering the telephone, or using a computer, and also includes all the lightbulbs that are on in the rooms you enter.

At the end of the day, review the electrical equipment you used. Rewrite your "My Electric Inventory" chart in your notebook, putting the items in three categories: Necessity, Convenience, or Luxury. (Be certain to leave room for one more column for the next activity.) Now add all the electrical equipment from your first list that you didn't use on your inventory day.

How did your actual use compare with your estimated use? Could you live without many of your electrical items? In the next activity you'll have a chance to try.

LEARN WHAT LIFE WAS LIKE BEFORE ELECTRICITY

Some electrical inventions have been around for a long time, such as lights and radios. Others were not as common when your parents were children, such as computers and cell phones. Perhaps they heard stories from their parents and grandparents about how people lived without as much electrical equipment as we have today.

Goal: *Research the past and discover old ways of doing things.*

Materials

* Notebook
* "My Electric Inventory" chart from previous activity
* Pencil

Directions

Add an "alternate" column to your "My Electric Inventory" chart. Show the list to your parents, grandparents, and other adults. Ask them how people did things without the electrical equipment you found in your house. Write their responses in this column. Try to discover a nonelectrical alternative for everything on your list. You might remember books you've read or movies you've seen about life long ago.

Discuss all your alternatives with your family or classmates. Did you find alternatives for everything? How did the alternatives make people's lives different from yours? Was life better in any way? Was it worse? Which electrical inventions would you miss most? Which would you not miss very much?

SPEND A DAY WITHOUT ELECTRIC POWER

Plan this activity when you don't have school, so you can spend the whole day without electricity. Talk to your family about doing this activity together so that you'll experience the full impact of using no electricity around the house. Even if they don't all agree to do it, do your best to stay away from those watts! (Note: Leave your electric refrigerator or freezer running, or the food will begin to spoil. But try to eat food that needs no refrigeration.)

Goal: Experience what life was like before electricity.

Materials

* Notebook
* Pencil

Directions

Spend a day without using electric power. Unplug your electric clock the night before you do this activity and take off your battery watch. (Remember, battery-powered items use electricity, even though they're not plugged into a wall socket.) Use a windup clock or watch, or try to tell time by the sun. Pay attention to everything you do. Don't turn on the lights and don't cook toast in the toaster. Try not to eat food from the refrigerator. (Discuss this with your parents first.)

Keep a diary during the day. Write about everything you do. Was it fun or hard work? Did it take longer to accomplish tasks without electricity? Which ones? Choose some nonelectrical activities for part of the day—playing sports, riding your bike, or reading by daylight. See how many nonelectrical alternatives you can use (see "Learn What Life Was Like Before Electricity"). If you have a gas oven, bake cookies using a hand beater. Wash the dishes by hand. Try some hand sewing (see the activities in chapter 5). Do some household chores without electricity. Wash your clothes by hand and hang them out to dry or clean your room without a vacuum cleaner.

What can you do after dark without electricity? Will you go to bed at sunset or light candles? (Check with your parents about using candles safely.) Make your own music or tell your own stories instead of listening to a radio or watching television. Play nonelectronic games, such as checkers or chess.

On the following day, discuss with other members of your family who participated in this activity how the day went. Write down everyone's answers to the following questions: Was it hard to live without electricity for a day? What parts were the most fun? Most difficult? Could you live comfortably without electricity for very long? How would your life change if you did? What things would be better? Worse?

In the next chapter, you'll learn to measure the electricity your family uses and find ways to conserve, or use less, electricity.

8
Wind Power Today

When you stand by the roadside near a wind turbine, you hear a soft *whoosh...whoosh...whoosh* as the giant blades turn hundreds of feet above you. The wind turning those turbines whips your hair across your face. Undulating grasses surround the towers and cattle graze beneath them. They are placidly unaware that the world's fastest growing energy industry is sharing their pasture. Those massive blades that revolve above them are generating electricity and helping to heal our planet.

Back in the 1970s many people grew worried about environmental problems and oil shortages. They began to look for new sources of energy and found an old one—wind power. No one expected the wind to run sawmills and grind grain the way it did in the Netherlands long ago. They wanted the wind to generate electricity for industry, homes, and even cars.

These new wind machines acquired a new name—wind turbines—and in 2010 they generated enough electricity in the United States to power 10 million homes. Europe's wind turbines generated over twice as much. And in 2010 China overtook the United States as the single country with the most installed wind power capacity.

Is wind a good energy source for generating electricity? Yes!

And it's getting better all the time.

Are these huge moving sculptures? No, they are the latest version of an old idea: using wind power to improve our lives. These wind turbines in northern California stand 250 feet tall, with 150-foot blades spinning in a 300-foot circle.

Gretchen Woelfle

What's New in the Wind

Wind technology has changed a lot since the 1970s. Inventors and engineers have experimented with different materials. They have changed the number and shape of the blades, invented new generators, tried many different-sized turbines, and added electronic components. Learning from their trials and errors, they have created wind turbines that are bigger and more efficient than ever. And they are still working at it.

Most turbines operate within a certain wind-speed range. Under eight miles per hour the blades don't generate electricity. At about 55 mph the flow of wind against the blades may be strong enough to damage the blades. In that case the blades begin to "feather," or twist so that the wind blows through them. This allows the turbine to

TOP 10 CUMULATIVE CAPACITY DEC 2010

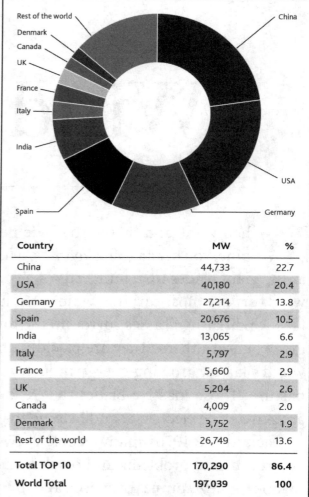

Country	MW	%
China	44,733	22.7
USA	40,180	20.4
Germany	27,214	13.8
Spain	20,676	10.5
India	13,065	6.6
Italy	5,797	2.9
France	5,660	2.9
UK	5,204	2.6
Canada	4,009	2.0
Denmark	3,752	1.9
Rest of the world	26,749	13.6
Total TOP 10	**170,290**	**86.4**
World Total	**197,039**	**100**

Back in the 1970s and 1980s, the United States led the world in wind-generated electricity. Today China has overtaken the United States, with European countries not too far behind. India may close the gap in years to come.

© *Global Wind Energy Council, Global Wind Report 2011*

spin more slowly and protect itself from damaging winds.

Like the old Dutch windmills, contemporary wind turbines come in different sizes. Models with **rotor** diameters as small as five feet are sold to rural homeowners to generate power in their own backyards. Turbines built for off-shore **wind farms** in the ocean are often larger than those found on land. Since the wind is usually much stronger offshore, turbines are being installed with blades 200 feet long.

How Efficient Is Wind Power?

You can judge a turbine's reliability in two ways. The first is how much of the time a turbine is available to generate electricity. With regular maintenance, a wind turbine will be ready to work more than 95 percent of the time. This is as good as, or better than, fossil fuel or nuclear power plants. And even when one wind turbine needs repairs, the others in the wind farm are up and running.

The second measurement is how much time turbines are generating electricity. As windmillers have always known, the wind is changeable. However, at windy places a wind turbine will generate electricity for nearly 6,000 hours per year, or almost two-thirds of the time. Because the wind is ever variable, the amount of power generated is also variable. However, compared to turbines installed in the 1980s, today's turbines generate much more electricity in the same amount of wind. The wind isn't blowing harder now, but engineers have learned how to capture more wind with the turbines and thus generate more electric power.

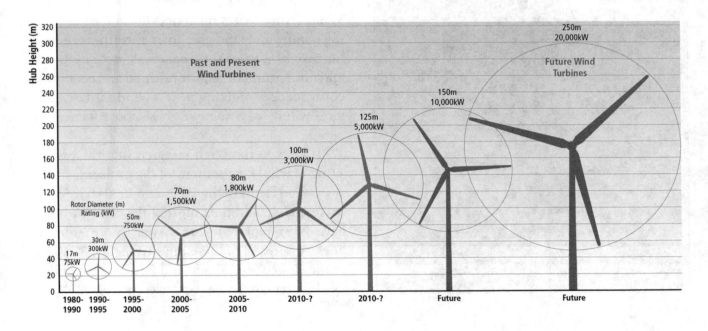

As wind turbines get bigger, they become more efficient. Look at the figures for a 50 m (164-foot) and 100 m (328-foot) turbine. Although the second turbine is twice as large, it generates four times as much electricity. The huge turbines of the future will most likely be installed offshore, in the ocean.

IPCC 2012: Special Report on Renewable Energy Sources and Climate Change Mitigation, Prepared by Working Group III of the Intergovernmental Panel on Climate Change, Figure 7.6

77

The wind blows strongest on the top of smooth, rounded hills, across open plains, near shorelines, and between mountain gaps. Hills, trees, lakes, and other landscape features affect wind speed too. Turbines themselves change wind patterns. If turbines are placed too close together, they can steal each other's wind. Wind farm developers track the wind for several years before installing turbines at the best sites to capture the most wind. This allows the machines to operate more often and produce more electricity.

This steer pays no attention to the wind turbines nearby. Ninety-eight percent of this ranch land is still used for grazing. Only 2 percent is needed for roads to the turbines and the turbines themselves.
Gretchen Woelfle

But wind speed is only one thing to consider. How close are transmission lines to the wind farm? Wind-generated electricity must be carried to the people who need it. Building wind farms where people live solves this problem. But many windy places are far from big cities. Building long-distance power lines can cost more than the turbines themselves. Birds and livestock are another concern. Is the site on a flyway for migrating birds? These issues must be addressed before a wind turbine is installed.

The 21st-Century Wind Farm

Wind farm developers will study a site for several years. Geologists, meteorologists, engineers, computer scientists, and naturalists also pitch in to see if an area will work well as a wind farm. Local communities are part of these studies too. Wind farm owners must obey local laws regarding zoning and land use. Town meetings are held for people to voice their concerns, ask questions, and understand the environmental and economic consequences of living near a wind farm. Chapter 9 will discuss some of these consequences in detail.

Thanks to thorough research into the proper siting of wind farms, many of the problems of the early wind farms in the 1970s and 1980s have been overcome. In addition, most of the older turbines have been replaced with newer, more efficient ones. As a result of these improvements, 38 states in the United States had wind farms that supplied local power companies with electricity in 2010.

Texas led the field with over 10,000 **megawatts** (MW) produced—enough power for 2.5 million households. But Iowa led in percentage of power generated by the wind. Between 15 and 20 percent of all Iowa electricity was generated from wind power. North Dakota and Minnesota were not far behind. And nearly everyone agrees that the wind is blowing in the right direction; 89 percent of American voters—Republicans, Democrats, and Independents—think we should generate even more electricity from wind power.

Wind Farms at Sea

Offshore wind turbines are turning in the brisk wind of nine European countries, and turbines will soon rise up off the Massachusetts coast in the United States. New Jersey, Maryland, and Virginia may be next. Large-scale offshore projects are going up off the coast of England, Scotland, and Japan. Wind farms at sea offer two big advantages. Offshore wind resources are vast, and they are close to heavily populated coastal areas, a major market for electrical power.

But wind turbines at sea cost more to install and operate. They need deep concrete bases built underwater, and routine maintenance can mean a boat trip in rough weather. Inventors are working on floating wind turbines, which would solve the problem of offshore platforms. In any case, larger offshore turbines, with 200-foot blades, spinning in heavy winds can provide large amounts of clean renewable energy.

The wind generally blows harder at sea than on land, and wind farms are being built in shallow water off the coast. These turbines are located in Liverpool Bay in the north of England. *NREL/DOE*

All Around the World

The good news about wind energy has spread all around the world. India and Mexico are building more wind farms all the time. Wind energy projects are cropping up in Japan, China, and South Korea, and turbine manufacturing plants continue to expand there.

What's Ahead in 2020 or 2030 or 2050?

Back in 1997 the European Commission set an annual target of 40,000 megawatts (or 40 gigawatts) of wind-generated electricity to be reached by 2010. Instead, 2010 saw over twice as much, and there are plans for triple that amount by 2020. An even more ambitious European plan envisions

Traditional farming activities continue in India as that country joins the race to use renewable wind energy to generate electricity.

producing all of its electrical power—that's 100 percent!—from renewable sources by 2050, with half, or 50 percent, generated by the wind.

And what about the United States? A 2008 Department of Energy study reported that it will be possible to generate 20 percent of our electricity with wind power by 2030. This is not an official government policy dedicated to making it happen, but a scientific study showing how it could be done. A target of 20 percent by 2030 is ambitious. What would that wind power landscape look like?

> Eight times more wind-generated electricity than in 2010
> Forty-six states producing substantial wind power
> New and improved transmission lines for all energy sources

What will all this cost? According to the Department of Energy study, about 50 cents per family per month.

Why Bother with Wind?

Wind-generated power will never be our only source of electricity, partly because wind speed is variable. But achieving 20 percent by 2030 offers many benefits too important to ignore. Those wind farms would reduce annual emissions of greenhouse gases by 825 tons (see chapter 9). Also, up to 500,000 new jobs could be created to build, maintain, and support the wind power

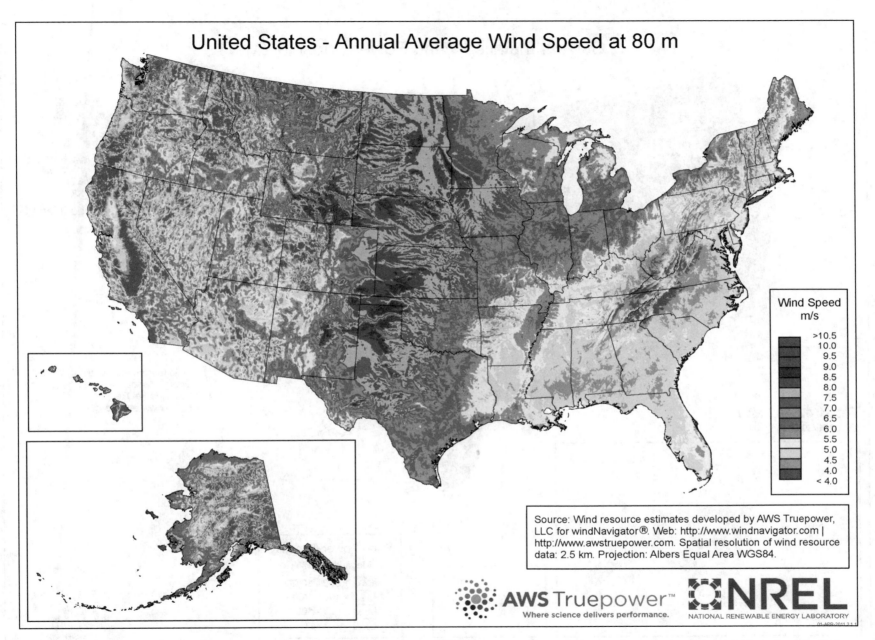

United States - Annual Average Wind Speed at 80 m

Wind Speed m/s

>10.5
10.0
9.5
9.0
8.5
8.0
7.5
7.0
6.5
6.0
5.5
5.0
4.5
4.0
< 4.0

Source: Wind resource estimates developed by AWS Truepower, LLC for windNavigator®. Web: http://www.windnavigator.com | http://www.awstruepower.com. Spatial resolution of wind resource data: 2.5 km. Projection: Albers Equal Area WGS84.

AWS Truepower™
Where science delivers performance.

NREL
NATIONAL RENEWABLE ENERGY LABORATORY

The wind blows strongly enough in many parts of the United States to generate 20 percent of our electricity by 2030. The shaded and dark areas offer the best sites for wind farms. The Great Plains are especially blustery, as the pioneers discovered. Other breezy areas include coastal regions, the Great Lakes, and mountain ranges. *NREL/DOE*

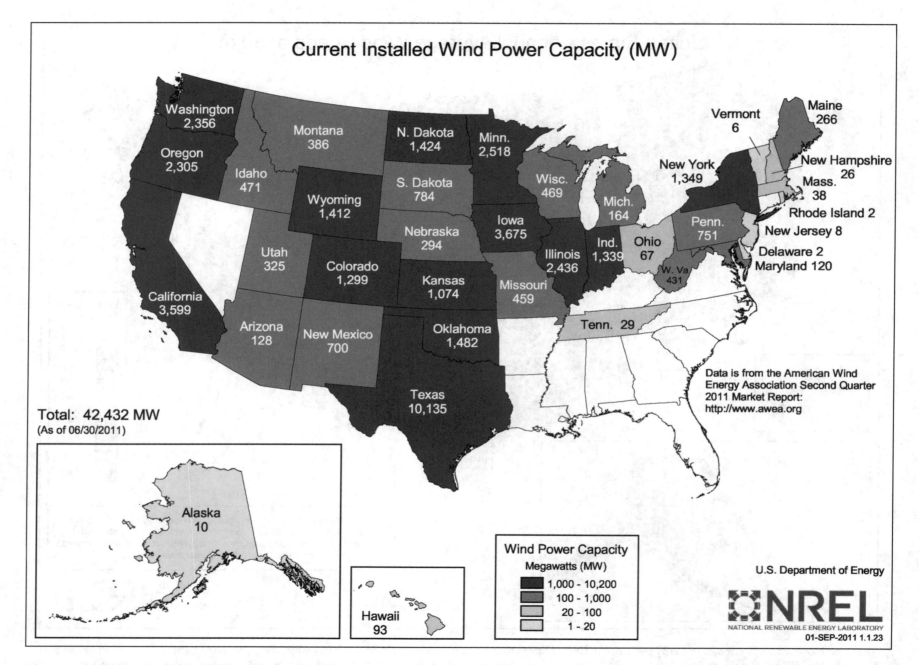

Current Installed Wind Power Capacity (MW)

Washington 2,356
Oregon 2,305
Idaho 471
Montana 386
N. Dakota 1,424
Minn. 2,518
Vermont 6
Maine 266
New Hampshire 26
New York 1,349
Wisc. 469
S. Dakota 784
Wyoming 1,412
Mich. 164
Penn. 751
Mass. 38
Rhode Island 2
New Jersey 8
Delaware 2
Maryland 120
Utah 325
Nebraska 294
Iowa 3,675
Ind. 1,339
Ohio 67
W. Va 431
California 3,599
Colorado 1,299
Kansas 1,074
Illinois 2,436
Missouri 459
Arizona 128
New Mexico 700
Oklahoma 1,482
Tenn. 29
Texas 10,135

Total: 42,432 MW
(As of 06/30/2011)

Alaska 10

Hawaii 93

Data is from the American Wind Energy Association Second Quarter 2011 Market Report: http://www.awea.org

Wind Power Capacity
Megawatts (MW)
1,000 – 10,200
100 – 1,000
20 – 100
1 – 20

U.S. Department of Energy

NREL
NATIONAL RENEWABLE ENERGY LABORATORY
01-SEP-2011 1.1.23

This map shows the states' installed capacity. Compare this map to the US wind map on the previous page to see how wind farms are flourishing in the windiest areas. When more offshore wind farms are built in the coming years, you'll see more dark shades along the coastlines. *NREL/DOE*

The image contains a diagram with the following labels: Pitch, Low-speed shaft, Gear box, Generator, Anemometer, Rotor, Controller, Wind Direction, Brake, Yaw Drive, Wind vane, Nacelle, Yaw motor, High-speed shaft, Blades, Tower.

industry. Because wind energy is "homegrown," the nation wouldn't depend as much on foreign sources of fossil fuels. And because the fuel—wind—is free, we wouldn't have to worry about rising prices and dwindling supply.

The Biggest Challenge

Since 20 percent by 2030 is a long-term goal, long-term plans are needed. The biggest obstacle the United States faces in achieving 20 percent by 2030 is the lack of a long-term government policy for renewable energy. Oil, coal, and natural gas industries get permanent federal support in the form of tax incentives (reduced taxes) for companies that invest in drilling and mining. But renewable energy, including wind power, has to live with the uncertainty of short-term support.

For many years Congress has approved tax incentive programs for renewable energy that last one or two years. It takes longer than this to develop a wind farm. The necessary steps include finding a suitable site; negotiating with landowners, local governments, and public utilities; hiring contractors, builders, and turbine suppliers; raising all the money for the work; and erecting the turbines.

In 2010 half of the states had laws in place that required electric companies to buy some of their power from renewable sources. This is helpful to the wind energy industry. But a supportive policy from the federal government has helped to get wind farms up and running.

Some wind experts would prefer no subsidies at all—for any energy source. Instead they favor feed-in tariffs, also called renewable energy rates.

(*left*) Hundreds of skilled workers are needed to install a new wind farm. When the turbines are up and running, permanent maintenance workers remain to keep them operating.
Mortenson Canada Corporation/ CanWEA Photo Gallery

(*right*) Wind turbines have many parts, but their workings are fairly simple. The blades turn in the wind. They are connected to a shaft that turns a generator, which makes electricity. The current is sent through cables down the turbine tower and underground to a transformer.
NREL/DOE

The desert mountains near Tehachapi, California, served as a testing ground for wind farms back in the 1970s and 1980s. Today these state-of-the-art turbines—much bigger and more efficient—are generating electricity in the same region to serve customers from San Diego to Los Angeles.
Iberdrola Renewables

but hasn't been adopted on a large scale in North America yet.

Coming of Age in California

The 1849 Gold Rush put California on the map. Few of those prospectors traveling through windy passes would have imagined that 200 years later the wind would also prove to be a precious resource. In the 1970s some of the first wind farms were erected in the Tehachapi-Mojave area of southern California, one of the windiest spots in North America. Today it is the site of the largest wind energy contract signed to date with a US utility.

Southern California Edison (SCE) has put its faith and its money in wind power, and has signed a 20-year contract to buy electricity from wind farms in the region. Key to the success of this project has been the construction of SCE's Tehachapi Renewable Transmission Project (TRTP). These power lines will transmit wind-generated electricity to millions of customers in southern California. The TRTP and the 20-year contract are likely to attract even more wind farms. Officials predict that the Tehachapi-Mojave region may eventually include 2,000 turbines.

Before TRTP, the wind industry in the area had stalled because existing transmission lines couldn't handle any more electricity. Now the area is likely to become the largest wind project in size and output in the country. The SCE TRTP took years of planning on the local, regional, and state levels. Five studies were carried out to find

These tariffs, or rates, are the price the state or national government sets for various energy producers—coal, wind, solar, etc. A feed-in tariff is not a tax incentive, or a subsidy to build a wind farm, but a guarantee to pay the turbine owners a set price for the electricity they generate. The system of feed-in tariffs is common in Europe,

the right solution for all parties concerned. Such large-scale, long-term planning is needed to get to 20 percent by 2030, and the Tehachapi-Mojave project can serve as a model.

The early wind turbines erected in this region were 60 feet off the ground and produced about 60 **kilowatts** (kW). Nearly all of these have been replaced by towers and turbines standing up to 400 feet tall and producing up to 2.4 MW—400 times as much electricity. Wind power has come of age in the little town of Tehachapi, California.

What Does Wind Power Cost?

A well-placed wind turbine can generate electricity for about 4.5 to 6 cents per kilowatt-hour (kWh). Installing a new wind farm costs about the same as building a new fossil-fuel-powered generating station. Old coal- and natural-gas-powered plants are cheaper to run if you count the cost of power generation alone. However, we are paying another price for our energy—an environmental price. This is a cost we cannot ignore.

Measuring Electrical Power
A (amps) × V (volts) = W (watts)
100W lightbulb burning 30 minutes uses 50W hours
100W lightbulb burning 1 hour uses 100W hours
1,000W = 1 kW (kilowatt)
1 kW × 1 hour = 1 kWh (kilowatt-hour)
1,000,000W × 1 hour = 1 MWh (megawatt-hour)
1,000,000,000W × 1 hour = 1 TWh (terawatt-hour)

Your family's electricity bill shows how many kilowatt-hours you use. Utility plants measure power in megawatts. The annual production of wind farms is measured in **terawatt**-hours.

LEARN HOW MUCH ELECTRICITY YOU USE

Goal: *Read your electric bill and meter to understand how much energy you use.*

Materials

* Electric bills from the past year, one for each season
* Calculator
* Graph paper
* Pencil
* Stool (optional)
* Flashlight (optional)
* Notebook

Directions

Look at your family's electricity bills from the previous year. (If necessary, you can probably order duplicate copies from your electric company online.) The categories on your bill may not have the same names as those illustrated on the next page, but you should find the same information.

How much electricity—in kilowatt-hours—does your family use each year? Calculate a daily average by taking the total monthly reading and dividing it by the number of days in that month.

Draw a graph on a sheet of graph paper, like the one shown on page 89, to record your family's use of kilowatt-hours. Mark a range of kilowatt-hours on the vertical axis and the names of the months on the horizontal axis. Do you use more electricity in different seasons? Why? Look at your list of electrical equipment in the activity called "Make an Electric Inventory of Your House" in the previous chapter to see what might make the difference.

Now measure how much electricity you are using today. Find your electric meter, which should look like the one pictured on the left. It may be outside, in the basement, or in a hallway. You may need a stool or a flashlight to see the meter. If you live in an apartment building, there may be many meters, one for each unit. Check the number on the meter to see that it matches the meter number on your electric bill.

(activity continued on page 88)

Metropolitan Electric Company

The *meter number* on your bill will match the number on your electric meter.

Customer and Service Address	Account #
Jane Consumer 1153 Palm Road Sun Valley, CA 91234	410-66823-01153-0008

Billing period or *service dates* refer to the time that you were charged for electric power. Each bill may cover one or two months.

Dates of Service   8/1/13–8/31/13

Energy used or *energy charged* will tell you how many kilowatt-hours (kWh) you used during this time period, the basic charge per kilowatt-hour, and the total cost of your electricity.

Current Electricity Rate

Service charge	$0.60
Energy used 553 kWh × $0.07288	$40.30
City tax 10%	$4.03
State tax 553 kWh × 0.00020	$0.11
Total	$45.04

City and state taxes and other charges may be added to your bill.

Meter Usage Information

Current Reading	Previous	Usage
21230	20677	553

The *usage comparison* section tells you how many kilowatt-hours your family used this year and last year during the same months. Also, it will give the average daily use and the seasonal average for both years.

Usage Comparison

Usage		Daily Average		Seasonal Average	
This year	Last year	This year	Last year	Summer	Winter
553 kWh	699 kWh	9 kWh	12kWh	10.4 kWh	19.6 KWh

LEARN HOW MUCH ELECTRICITY YOU USE *continued*

An electric meter has a wheel in the center. The faster the wheel rotates, the more electricity you are using at that moment. Watch how fast the meter turns. Walk through your house and see how many electrical items are on (lights, television, and so on). Turn off anything that is not needed. Look at your meter again and see if the wheel is spinning more slowly.

The five dials on the meter turn at different speeds and show the number of kilowatt-hours used. In your notebook, create a chart like the one in the next activity (page 90). Read your meter and then write down the numbers on the dials from left to right. Look at the one on the extreme left. Is the dial pointing directly to a number? Write down that number. If the pointer is between two numbers, write down the *lower* number. Read the dial to the right in the same way and record it to the right of the first number. Continue reading the dials and writing the numbers.

Look at your latest electricity bill. How many days have passed since the last official meter reading? What was the kilowatt-hour reading then? Subtract this amount from your reading. Is it more or less than the last billing period? Can you explain the change?

Check out www.epa.gov/climatechange/emissions/ind_calculator .html to calculate the greenhouse gas emissions produced in generating the electricity you use.

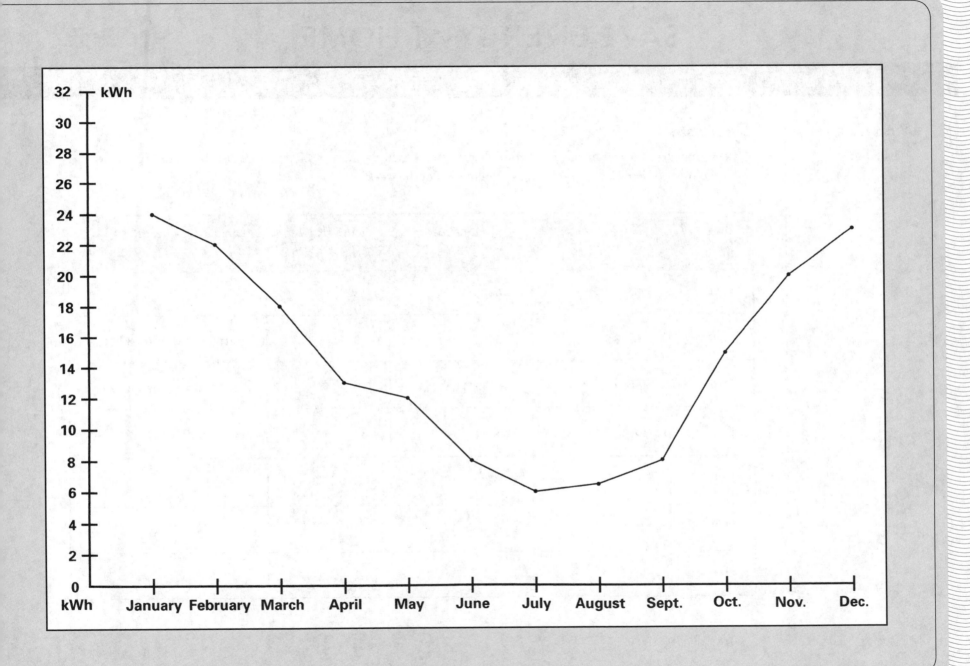

SAVE ENERGY AT HOME

Goal: *Monitor your electricity use and change your energy habits to conserve electricity.*

Materials

* Notebook
* Pencil

Directions

Make a chart like the one below. Read your electric meter each day for a week (see page 86). Try to determine why you used more or less electricity during different days of the week.

Date	Current Meter Reading	Previous Meter Reading	Kilowatt-Hours Used	Special Activities
11/4	16698	16685	13	
11/5	16723	16698	25	portable heater on 8 hours
11/6	16739	16723	16	lights and TV on all day
11/7	16747	16739	8	away all day
11/8				
11/9				
11/10				

Call a family meeting and talk about using less electricity. Look on your electric company's website for information about energy conservation programs. Share these conservation ideas with your family. Create a plan for your family to modify their electricity use by doing things like turning off lights when leaving a room, turning off the television, and more. You may save a few dollars a month on your electricity bill. Each family's energy habits do make a difference.

After putting this energy-saving plan into action, read the electric meter each day for another week and record the results. Call another family meeting and review your findings. Are you using less electricity? Does everyone agree that you are as energy efficient as you can be? If the answer to both questions is yes, congratulate yourselves. If you think you can be more energy efficient, review your conservation plan and keep trying. The following ideas may help.

Hints for Conserving Energy

> In the winter, lower your thermostat a few degrees to save heat and put on a sweater instead. If you use air conditioning in the summer, keep your house a few degrees warmer than usual to save energy. Do you need to heat or cool every room in the house all day long? Is it possible to close some air vents in rooms you aren't using?

> Insulate your home (walls, windows, doorways) and your hot water heater to save on heating and cooling costs. (Your power company may pay part or all of the costs of these conservation measures.)

> Turn your refrigerator dial to a warmer setting to save energy.

> Turn lights off when no one is in the room.

> Turn computers, televisions, cell phone chargers, and other electronic equipment off at the plug when you are not using them. Even "stand-by mode" uses electricity.

> Don't use the heated drying setting on your dishwasher. This doubles the amount of energy it takes to do the dishes.

> Hang your clothes out to dry on a sunny and windy day. Your clothesline is a solar- and wind-powered dryer!

> Many new models of electrical equipment—including that energy hog, the refrigerator—use much less electricity than older models. When it's time to buy a new appliance or piece of electronic equipment, compare the energy use of different models. (Some appliances offer energy cost/savings charts affixed to their exterior.)

> Try compact fluorescent lightbulbs. They cost more to buy, but they use much less electricity and last 10 to 20 times longer than ordinary incandescent lightbulbs. In the long run, they are much cheaper and more energy efficient. Also, your electricity company may give special rebates for compact fluorescent bulbs.

9

A Solution in the Wind

THREE-YEAR DROUGHT CONTINUES
RIVERS CREST AND THREATEN SEVERE FLOODING
HURRICANE DEVASTATES COASTAL REGION
HOTTEST SUMMER ON RECORD, DEATH TOLL RISES

Headlines like these used to be rare. Today, extreme weather is a common event. That's because the global climate is changing. The earth is getting warmer, the ice at the poles is melting, glaciers all over the world are disappearing, and sea levels are beginning to rise. The period from 2000 to 2009 was the warmest decade since scientists started keeping records in 1850.

Scientists predict that wet regions will probably get wetter and dry regions will probably get drier. Droughts, storms, and heat waves are likely to become more severe, and weather everywhere will become less predictable. Some of today's farmland may become too arid to grow food, and drought may lead to more forest fires. The delicate balance of ecosystems—plants, animals, habitat, and climate—is already being disrupted.

Global Warming Has Arrived

Over the last two centuries fossil fuels have powered the factories that manufacture the goods that we use all day long. Oil, refined as gasoline and other fuels, runs automobiles and airplanes. Natural gas heats our homes and cooks our food. And coal, oil, and natural gas generate

(*left*) In 2011 the Souris River inundated Minot, North Dakota, and damaged surrounding cropland. Climate change is causing unpredictable weather all over the world. Some places will receive more rain and more flooding.

US Geological Survey Photo Library

(*right*) This Texas farmer shows his drought-stricken land to a soil scientist from the Natural Resources Conservation Service. Severe drought has hit many regions of the world as global warming advances.

US Department of Agriculture

most of the electricity that lights up our lives. But our conveniences carry a price.

When coal, oil, and natural gas are burned, they give off carbon dioxide and other gases that rise high into the atmosphere. A layer of these gases prevents some of the earth's heat from escaping back into space. These are called greenhouse gases, because they act like a glass greenhouse, trapping heat and making the earth warmer. There has been a 25 percent rise in atmospheric carbon dioxide since 1860.

In 2007 the Intergovernmental Panel on Climate Change (IPCC), sponsored by the United Nations, published a 2,900-page report. The report was researched and written by scientists from 19 national academies of science throughout the world and endorsed by many other independent scientific groups. The IPCC report, the most comprehensive summary of current climate research, came to the following conclusions:

> ❯ The climate is undergoing a pronounced warming trend, beyond the range of normal variations

> ❯ The major cause of the warming is rising levels of the greenhouse gas carbon dioxide (CO_2)

> ❯ The rise in CO_2 is the result of burning fossil fuels

> ❯ If CO_2 levels continue to rise, the warming will continue

> ❯ The resulting climate change presents a danger to human welfare and the environment

Although scientists don't agree on all the details, they agree that climate change is happening, we're causing it, and it's not a good thing. According to the IPCC report, to avoid the worst effects of climate change, global greenhouse gas emissions must begin to decline before 2020.

Solutions All Around

The good news is that we can do something about reducing these emissions. Hundreds of books, websites, television programs, and films are presenting the problems and solutions surrounding climate change. Wind power is one of the solutions.

Forty percent of greenhouse gas emissions come from generating electricity. Wind turbines emit no greenhouse gases. A wind turbine has a three-to-six-month "payback time"—the time it takes for a turbine to generate as much energy as it took to manufacture and install it. For the rest of its 20-year life span the turbine is generating 100 percent pollution-free power.

The more electricity we generate from wind energy and other renewable sources, the less fossil fuels we will have to burn. Another solution is energy conservation. See the activities at the end of the previous chapter (page 86) for more information on saving energy in your home.

The Health Costs of Coal

Two-thirds of US electricity is generated by burning coal. Each year, over 386,000 tons of 84 toxic air pollutants are released into the air by

coal-burning power plants in 46 of the 50 states. People living close to these plants suffer most from the pollution, but airborne chemicals travel hundreds and even thousands of miles, affecting the health of many more people.

The US Environmental Protection Agency (EPA) estimates that every year exposure to coal-plant pollutants in the United States

> causes 17,000 deaths

> causes 11,000 heart attacks

> causes 120,000 childhood asthma attacks

Plug-in hybrid electric vehicles, like this car, have an electric motor and an internal combustion engine. When the electric charge runs out, the gasoline engine takes over. To recharge the battery, just plug it into an electric outlet at home. When your electricity is generated by wind turbines or solar panels, as shown here, you've got a truly ecological ride!
NREL/DOE

(*left*) Generating electricity by burning coal creates pollutants that damage the health of humans and the environment. Today the cost of wind-powered electricity is comparable to coal-powered electricity. It's time to turn toward the wind!

John Fowler, Photographer

(*right*) Open-pit coal mining creates environmental havoc. It poisons rivers and lakes and destroys habitat for plants and animals. Villages and towns are polluted, often beyond repair. Forests that absorb greenhouse gases are destroyed, which adds to global warming. Compare that to wind power—a free, clean, renewable energy source.

Bureau of Land Management Photos

Cleaning up coal-burning power plants will cost money and possibly raise the price of electricity for many people. But what is the cost of those illnesses and deaths? It is impossible to measure their value in dollars and cents, but they should be considered when we decide how to generate electricity.

The Environmental Cost of Fossil Fuels

Fossil fuels are damaging not only to human health but to the earth as well. Mining coal by "mountaintop removal" is an ecological disaster. In Appalachia 2,000 miles of streams have been poisoned and millions of tons of waste rock have been dumped into valleys below, causing permanent damage to the ecosystem. Oil spills have caused massive damage to the ocean and its inhabitants.

Given the many harmful environmental effects of fossil fuels—from those caused by extracting them from the earth to their damaging residues high in the atmosphere—renewable forms of energy make sense. We cannot replace fossil fuels completely—no other current source of fuel could lift a giant airliner off the ground. But we could generate much of our electricity without fossil fuels.

Renewable Energy Sources

Various renewable energy sources are less polluting than fossil fuels, but they have disadvantages too. Hydropower projects involve damming rivers to create lakes, then using falling water to turn turbines and generate electricity. This radically alters the ecology of dammed rivers and threatens its wildlife. Also, the organic matter in the flooded lands behind the dam decomposes and releases methane, a greenhouse gas that traps 25 times more heat than carbon dioxide.

Solar power is a growing industry. Some people are putting photovoltaic panels on their roofs to heat water and generate their own electricity. Large solar farms are being built in desert regions like California and Arizona, as well as sunny countries like Spain and even cloudy places like Germany. These solar farms require more land than an equivalent wind farm, and costs for generating solar electricity are higher than those for wind energy. But solar power should play an important role in our energy future because, like the wind, solar energy is 100 percent renewable: we won't run out of it.

Protecting Birds

When large wind farms were first built back in the 1980s, few people considered their impact on birds. Then some wind farm operators found dead birds at the base of the turbine towers. The wind farm at Altamont Pass in Northern California turned out to be an especially dangerous place for birds.

Raptors—hawks, eagles, and other birds who hunt on the wing—populate Altamont Pass in large numbers, because of the hordes of rodents on the ground, their favorite prey. Raptors have

An explosion at the Deepwater Horizon oil-drilling platform in the Gulf of Mexico in April 2010 killed 11 people and triggered the worst oil spill ever. As US Coast Guard boats, shown here, battled a fire triggered on the drilling rig, oil gushed out of the underwater well. For three months oil poured into the Gulf of Mexico; nearly five billion barrels of oil spilled out before the well was capped. This had terrible economic consequences for fishermen and other workers. The ecological devastation to sea life caused by the oil spill has continued to grow. *US Coast Guard*

Solar power—the sun's energy—is another promising renewable energy source that may help fill our need for electricity. This array of photovoltaic (electricity-generating) solar panels covers 144 acres in the Arizona desert and produces enough electricity to power 3,700 homes. *Iberdrola Renewables*

keen vision and can see mice and other prey from high in the sky. But still they collide with turbines, and scientists aren't sure why. The blades are turning slowly enough for them to notice. Perhaps they are watching the ground, not the area in front of them as they circle through the air.

Old, smaller turbines pose the biggest threat to birds. Taller wind turbines installed today have greatly reduced bird fatalities, because most birds fly below the blades. Half of the older turbines at Altamont Pass are being replaced with fewer larger ones. This should decrease the number of birds killed. Of course, most birds don't collide with turbines. They simply fly around them. Hull, Massachusetts, has two large turbines in their town on the Atlantic coast. In 12 years of operation they have only found one dead seagull at the turbines.

Working Together

As with all innovations, wind farm developers are learning from experience, trial, and error to understand and fix the problems. Scientists are studying the impact of wind turbines on birds, bats, and other wildlife. They have found that problems involving wildlife and wind power can usually be solved by careful placement of the turbines. Field research can identify the migration routes, breeding grounds, or nesting sites of resident animals. Monitoring the wind farms after turbines are installed can identify the impact—positive, neutral, or negative—on wildlife.

The Audubon Society—a US bird conservation group—may oppose a particular wind farm project in certain sensitive areas, but it generally supports the use of wind energy, for the 2007 IPCC study reports that climate change poses a much greater threat to birds than wind farms do. Global warming has already impacted the survival of half of the world's bird species.

Scientists have also studied the impact of offshore wind turbines on marine life and water birds. Over 17 years, they found that fish, seals, and porpoises, as well as migrating birds, had no trouble living with the turbines. Some fish were even attracted to the underwater concrete foundations, using them as hatcheries or nursing grounds.

To reduce bird and bat deaths at wind turbines, scientists study the site before a wind farm is built. They learn the habits of local and migrating birds and avoid building in locations where collisions are likely to occur. Larger, taller turbines have also reduced bird deaths, for many birds fly below the turning blades.
© Arturoli

Wind Farm Opponents

Despite all their environmental benefits, some people oppose the construction of wind farms. Their main complaints are the sound and sight of turbines. Scientists measuring the sound of a wind turbine 1,000 feet away—about three football fields—found the level of noise to be about 50 decibels—halfway between a whisper and the noise inside a car (not including the music!) Since wind turbines are always located in windy areas, the wind itself may be louder than the turbines.

The American and Canadian Wind Energy Associations (AWEA and CanWEA) assembled a team of medical doctors, hearing specialists, and sound professionals to study all the scientific research on the health effects of living near wind turbines. The team of experts concluded that, though some people might not like it, there was no proof that the sound of a turbine was harmful to human health.

As for the look of the turbines, it's a matter of personal preference. Some people see them as sculptures in the landscape, blades slowly turning in the wind. Others like the look of them because of the clean energy they produce. They are a symbol of a greener future. But other people oppose them because they say they spoil the view.

Paul Gipe, who has been a wind power expert for many decades, thinks the opposition goes deeper than that, to a resistance, even fear, that people have of change. People are used to flicking a switch, paying a monthly bill, and never thinking about where their electricity comes from.

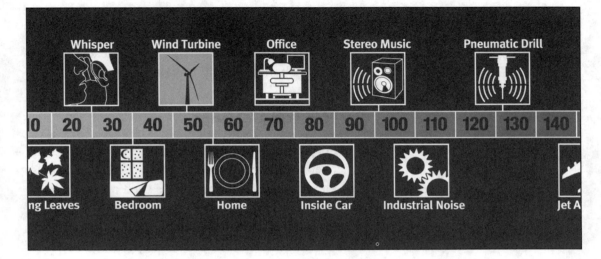

(*top*) This chart shows how the sound of a wind turbine located 1,000 feet away compares to the sounds of everyday life.
Canadian Wind Energy Association

(*left*) Some people like the way they look, others don't. But wind turbines make good sense for the economy and the environment, and we will see more of them in the future.
Gretchen Woelfle

Wind farms represent a new reality that challenges the old fossil-fuel-based system. What will this new renewable-energy reality lead to? How will it change our old way of life?

Resisting Change

Soon after Alexander Graham Bell invented the telephone back in 1876, the *New York World* newspaper asked, "Of what use is such an invention?" The men who financed Bell's research asked him to stop working on the telephone, for they couldn't see how it could make them any money.

Ten years later, when telephone lines started going up in cities and towns across the country, citizens cut them down in their front yards. In Oshkosh, Wisconsin, the mayor ordered police officers and firefighters to chop them down all over town. Newspapers called the poles and wires "an urban blight," and people thought them ugly. But towns and cities were already strung with unsightly telegraph lines, power lines, and trolley cables. The telephone poles were part of a new invention that would change people's lives and bring the outside world into the privacy of their homes. It changed the reality they were used to.

Wind farms today contain fewer, larger turbines than wind farms in the past, but still some people object. Public meetings are held to allow all opinions to be expressed during the planning stages. Then elected town councils decide whether to approve wind farms. The sight of a wind farm is one issue that they consider, the long-term economic impact on the town is another.

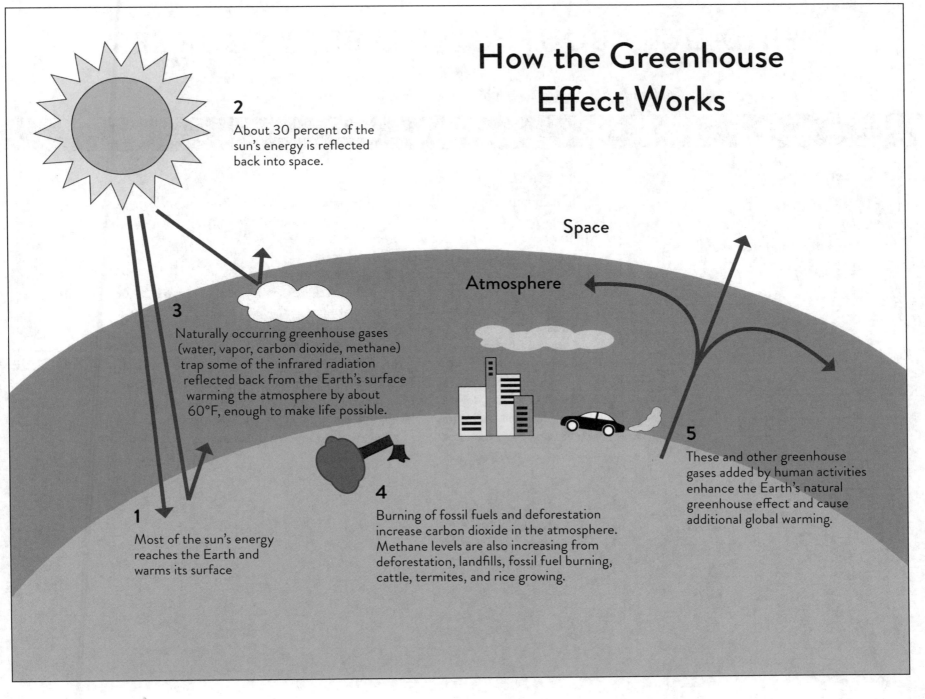

How the Greenhouse Effect Works

2
About 30 percent of the sun's energy is reflected back into space.

Space

Atmosphere

3
Naturally occurring greenhouse gases (water, vapor, carbon dioxide, methane) trap some of the infrared radiation reflected back from the Earth's surface warming the atmosphere by about 60°F, enough to make life possible.

1
Most of the sun's energy reaches the Earth and warms its surface

4
Burning of fossil fuels and deforestation increase carbon dioxide in the atmosphere. Methane levels are also increasing from deforestation, landfills, fossil fuel burning, cattle, termites, and rice growing.

5
These and other greenhouse gases added by human activities enhance the Earth's natural greenhouse effect and cause additional global warming.

FIND OUT ABOUT YOUR ENERGY SOURCES

You can do your part to help wind turbines and renewable energy fulfill their promise. You'll need to use the Internet, a telephone, and perhaps the library in this activity to locate information about the community in which you live.

Goal: *Increase your energy awareness by doing some investigative research on your local community and its elected officials.*

Materials

* Paper
* Pen
* Computer with Internet connection
* Telephone
* Library (optional)

Directions

Call the public affairs or community relations department of your local electrical utility company, or access their website, to find out how and where your electricity is generated. It may be all from one source or from several sources. If it comes from several sources, ask what percentage comes from each source.

On the Internet, find the website for the Energy Commission in your state or province and look for their renewable energy pages. Is there a policy or a target goal to use a certain percentage of renewable energy for generating electricity? If not, is there a movement to create such a policy or target goal? Find out the details.

On the Internet, research the energy bills that are being considered in Congress and your state legislature, including those that support renewable energy projects.

Find the names and addresses of your congressional and state representatives on the Internet or from a librarian. Try to find out how your representatives voted on energy bills in the past, including renewable energy bills. Write and ask them their views on bills coming up for a vote. Let them know your opinions on these issues.

TAKE ENVIRONMENTAL ACTION

Is your area suffering environmental damage from pollution or extreme weather conditions due to climate changes? All across the country people are working to improve or preserve their local environment.

Goal: Find out how you can help solve the environmental problems in your community.

Materials

* Paper
* Pen
* Computer with Internet connection
* Telephone
* Library (optional)

Directions

Check local newspapers online or in the library for articles on local environmental problems. Your local newspaper may have an environmental reporter that covers these issues. E-mail or call to interview him or her for more information.

Interview several people—your parents, neighbors, teachers, or librarians—to find out what they know about such conditions.

Find groups that are working on your local environmental problems. These may be found in the newspaper articles. Or check the websites of national environmental groups listed in the bibliography. Do they have chapters in your area?

Contact one or more of these groups. Do they give presentations to school groups? Can students help with ongoing community action projects? What other ways can you help?

10
Fulfilling the Promise

Family farms and ranches in North America are disappearing as owners find it hard to meet rising costs. Much of the farm and grazing land in the Midwest and West is windy enough for wind turbines, and growing numbers of farmers and ranchers have welcomed turbines on their land. The tower platforms take up little space, and crops and livestock can flourish underneath the whirling blades.

Many wind farm developers lease the land the turbines occupy, generally paying landowners about $5,000 or more per turbine per year. This is welcome income to farmers and ranchers. Iowa farmer Tim Hemphill said of his turbines, "I just think they are fantastic. I wish the whole farm were covered with them." They have helped him keep his farm in the family.

Tom Carr, a Colorado rancher, has also welcomed turbines. "It's a very small footprint that those turbines leave . . . We're not going to be grazing or housing any less cattle than before." But it's about more than money. Carr goes on, "I'm conservative by nature, but it's not about being a Democrat or Republican or Green Party member. We all have a vested interest in protecting our children and our children's children."

Wind farm companies pay taxes on the money they make from the electricity they sell. This boon allows rural towns to invest in improved schools, hospitals, and recreation facilities. The 2008 US Department of Energy report found that reaching 20 percent wind power by 2030 could bring $1.5 billion a year in taxes to local communities, and lease payments to rural landowners could top $600 million a year.

Today half of the wind turbine components installed in the United States are made in the United States, and this will likely increase in the future as the industry grows. From factory workers who make the components, to businessmen who develop wind farms, to naturalists who study wind farms and wildlife, to **windsmiths** who maintain them, to engineers and inventors working on new technology—wind energy offers a wide range of jobs.

Wind for Schools

Wind turbines are popping up in rural school yards across the country. These are part of the Wind for Schools Project, sponsored by the US Department of Energy and the National Renewable Energy Laboratory. While the turbine spins outside, inside students are building wind turbine models that really work.

One teacher said that Wind for Schools "allowed us to take a real life example of what's going on right here in Kansas. It allowed the kids to understand the science behind something that is changing our environment and our economy." The kids monitor the data from the turbine in their school yard to see how much energy is generated. The turbine generates more than a science unit in the classroom. It also generates electricity that saves the school money.

Meanwhile, at nearby Kansas State University, engineering students study the principles of wind turbines and learn how to analyze a possible site for a wind farm. Then they work with experts to build more Wind for Schools turbines. Both parts of the program are designed to create a workforce for the wind energy field. One engineering student said, "It's important that everyone starts learning about these renewable resources at a younger age." Who knows—perhaps one of those young students will go on to invent a new and better wind turbine!

Wind turbines on the farm are becoming common sights in midwestern and western North America. They give farmers and ranchers extra income, add tax money to the nearby towns, and generate clean green electricity.
Gretchen Woelfle

106

A Community Takes Charge

Hull, Massachusetts, a small town of 10,000 people, lies on the southern tip of Boston Harbor, where the wind blows off the Atlantic Ocean. Back in the 1820s two brothers built a windmill in Hull, and folks named the site Windmill Point. That windmill is long gone, but in 1985 the citizens of Hull built a wind turbine on the same spot, now the campus of Hull High School. For 12 years the turbine generated power for the school and saved the town $70,000 in electricity bills. Then a 70-mph windstorm damaged one of the blades and the turbine was taken down.

But the town was sold on wind power, and a group of teachers and other locals looked into installing a larger wind turbine. The high school physics class did some of the research and worked with the Hull Municipal Light Plant, which provides power to the town. Scientists from the University of Massachusetts led a thorough study of the project. Then in 2001 a new turbine, Hull 1, was installed, which generated 16 times more electricity than the old turbine.

And that's not the end of the story. In 2006 Hull 2 was installed at the other end of town. This turbine generates more than twice as much power as Hull 1! A third small turbine spins at the local Weir Estuary Nature Center. "The Hull experience shows it is easier to win approval for wind projects if the benefits are enjoyed close to home," said one local wind supporter. "We're the investors and we're the beneficiaries."

In 2007 Hull won the Department of Energy's Wind Power Pioneer Award for "outstanding

(*top*) These Denver, Colorado, high school students check their turbine blades before measuring the number of volts it can generate. The National Renewable Energy Laboratory runs education programs like these to attract students to clean-energy careers. *NREL/DOE*

(*left*) Children in Medford, Massachusetts, can see wind turbines in action at school. The Wind for Schools Project, sponsored by the US Department of Energy, installs turbines at schools from Alaska to Florida, and Maine to California. In their classroom, students learn how their wind turbine works. *NREL/DOE*

A wind turbine stands on the tip of land once called Windmill Point, in Hull, Massachusetts. This small town, just across the harbor from Boston, installed its first turbine in 1985 and now has two much bigger ones. Progress doesn't have to happen on a grand scale. It can come about one wind turbine at a time.
Hull Municipal Light Plant

companies are interested, and the Department of Energy has given Hull a grant to develop the project.

Richard Miller, the head of the Hull Municipal Light Plant, explains his own enthusiasm for wind energy. "I favor it not just because it's green, but because it makes good sense. We've kept electric rates stable for customers, and our rates are lower than some of the bigger power companies in the state."

Own Your Own Turbine

Schools and towns are buying wind turbines with the help of government grants and bank loans. And some communities are offering its residents a chance to get into the act. Can't afford to buy a turbine on your own? Perhaps your family and neighbors can buy a small part of one.

The community-based wind movement began in Denmark and Germany, where feed-in tariffs, also called renewable energy rates, have been established. These rates, set by the state or national government, allow communities to estimate in advance how much money they will make with their turbines.

Dan Juhl, founder of Juhl Wind in Woodstock, Minnesota, has developed dozens of community-based projects since the 1990s. "It's the best thing since the invention of the tractor for rural communities," he claims. When the local landowners own the turbines, more of the income and job benefits stay in the local community.

Juhl's community-based projects are financed by "the Minnesota flip structure."

leadership in advancing the use of wind power in a coastal community." The award committee declared that Hull had provided "a model for engaging the entire community to understand and move forward together on its wind power project, from school teachers, utility engineers and local leaders to state government, academia and industry."

For several years now, Hull has explored the possibility of installing wind turbines offshore. This is a complicated and expensive project. One issue, for example, is that no US ships are large enough to erect a turbine out at sea. But the people of Hull haven't given up. They want to build one turbine platform offshore as a research station so that companies can test different turbines and monitor the results. Several US and European

- Local landowners put up about 1 percent of the money needed to build one or more turbines. They may join together to build perhaps 10 to 20 turbines.

- The Juhl Wind company finds a corporate partner to finance 99 percent of the project.

- A contract is signed with a utility company to buy the wind-generated power at a fixed price.

- For the first 10 years the 99 percent partner gets federal tax credits and most of the income from the power generation.

- For the first 10 years the local owners receive a fee to operate their turbines. Their 1 percent investment is usually repaid in a year or two.

- After 10 years, the ownership "flips." Local owners own 99 percent of the turbines and receive 99 percent of the income for the life of the turbine.

With a community-based project, more energy dollars are kept in the community. Local citizens see and feel their investment in their own backyards, and there is much less opposition to wind farms. One turbine owner said, "I used to hate the wind. It blows your hat off. It blows the seed corn across the fields. It makes it impossible to spray. But now I love the wind!"

Looking beyond the local benefits, Dan Juhl declares that if we don't solve the long-term problem of energy independence, "what are we leaving our kids but a polluted mess?" Community-based wind farms are a patriotic solution to the problems of climate change. They are good for the community, the environment, and the country. Juhl often faces opposition from utility companies. They are often large monopolies that prefer to do business with large energy corporations who build large wind farms. But for Juhl the benefits of community-based wind projects are worth the fight.

Winter on the prairie doesn't stop this wind turbine from rising near Chandler, Minnesota. It is part of the Valley View community wind farm that is partly owned by farmers and townspeople. They helped to finance the project, and now they sell the power to their utility company and make money from the green power their wind turbines generate.
Juhl Wind Inc.

Tyler Juhl, Dan's son, is a wind technician who works on wind turbines. "It's a fulfilling job. You're working on clean green energy. It's a great feeling doing something that good."

Winds of Change

For decades now, the price of oil and gas has been unpredictable. Today we are beginning to see the economic effects of climate change. What will the price of fossil fuels be in the future? What will the final costs of climate change be? The answer to both questions is the same. We don't know.

What we do know is that wind energy has a stable and predictable cost. The technology is improving all the time and the fuel is plentiful and free, with virtually no environmental costs.

Wind power has brought about many changes over the centuries. The Dutch and their windmills drained and enlarged their country. North American windmills helped to transform the prairies into the breadbasket of the world. Modern wind turbines can help to fill our energy needs with clean, safe power, and they may help to save our planet.

There's good news blowing in the wind.

Nine Reasons Why Wind Power Is a Good Idea

1. The wind blows everywhere

2. There's a lot of it

3. We will never use it up

4. The fuel—wind—is free

5. Wind turbines don't use much land

6. Wind turbines don't create toxic emissions

7. Wind power doesn't use any water

8. Land beneath a wind turbine can be farmed or grazed

9. Installing a turbine doesn't take much time

Many promising careers await young men and women in the wind energy field. (See "Windmill Careers," page 125.) Some wind power workers, such as the engineers and scientists who plan and design wind farms, remain on the ground, while others, such as the wind technicians who service the turbines, work hundreds of feet in the air where the views are fantastic!

Scientists from the California Institute of Technology have set up an experimental wind farm with vertical axis turbines in the Antelope Valley, north of Los Angeles. They will monitor the turbines and the electricity they produce, and decide if this design has a future.

California Institute of Technology

Inventors haven't finished tinkering with wind turbines. Inspired by the flow physics of schools of fish, scientists at Cal Tech designed these experimental vertical axis turbines to work well when spaced close together. You may see these, and many other kinds of turbines, spinning in the wind in years to come.

California Institute of Technology

GLOBAL WIND DAY

Global Wind Day is celebrated every June 15 all around the world. Children and adults get together to learn something about the wind or just have fun—or both!

Goal: Join in the worldwide celebration of Global Wind Day.

Materials

✴ Internet access

✴ Costumes, kites, art materials, etc.

Directions

The website www.globalwindday.org describes all kinds of ways that people around the world celebrate Global Wind Day. Next June 15, you can plan your own celebration. Perhaps your school will sponsor it, or a local environmental group will help organize it at a local park. You can use the event to raise money for environmental organizations—or you can just have fun!

Here are a few ideas of how to celebrate:

❭ Visit a windmill or a wind turbine in your area (see "Where to Find Windmills," page 115).

❭ Dress up like an old-fashioned windmiller in breeches and smock, a cowboy windmiller, or a modern windmiller in a hardhat and jeans.

❭ Fly a kite.

❭ Organize a "Run Like the Wind" or "Cycle Like the Wind" event. It doesn't have to be a race. You could run or ride around a track, asking friends or family to sponsor you and donating the money to a local environmental group.

❭ Set up an arts-and-crafts booth where participants can make a windmill paper collage (page 48), a wind sock and wind vane (page 14), or one of the other creative activities in this book.

❭ Set up a "science fair" based on one of the scientific activities in this book—for instance, the projects in chapters 1 (page 6) and 2 (page 16)—and share your results with other participants.

❭ Invite a folksinger with guitar or banjo to lead a sing-along, with songs such as "Starving to Death on My Government Claim" (page 63) and "Blowin' in the Wind."

❭ Bake cookies or cupcakes and decorate the tops with a wind turbine symbol.

❭ Or . . . use your imagination to come up with other ways to celebrate wind power!

INVESTIGATE A WIND FARM

Wind farms of all sizes are popping up all over the world: from large numbers of huge turbines that sell power to public utility companies, to single turbines installed at a school or town.

Goal: Learn the different issues involved in siting a wind farm. (Adapted from AWEA's "10 Steps to Developing a Wind Farm" www.awea.org/_cs_upload/learnabout/publications/4141_1.pdf.)

Materials

* Computer with Internet connection
* Paper
* Pen
* Telephone
* Library (optional)

Directions

Choose an existing wind farm in your area or in another state. The state energy commission will most likely link to a map and a list of wind farms. Or choose a Wind for Schools site at www.windpoweringamerica.gov/schools/projects.asp. Research the wind resources of your chosen wind farm. For more detailed information see www.windpoweringamerica.gov/wind_maps.asp. If you can, travel to the site to see it, feel the wind, and learn how the land is being used. How far is your site from existing transmission lines? Contact the public utility company in the area to find out the location and carrying capacity of power lines.

Access to Land. Who owns the land your wind farm is on? Is it public or private land? If it's private, does the wind farm company own it or do they lease it from farmers or ranchers? Do wind turbines fit in with the existing use of the land?

Identify a market for your wind-generated electricity. Does the state require utilities to buy electricity from wind farms or other renewable sources? Has it reached its target goal yet? AWEA state fact sheets will help you here: www.awea.org/learnabout/publications/factsheets/factsheets_state.cfm.

Address other issues about the site. Are there endangered or protected species living on or near the site? Is it a flyway for migrating birds? How has the local community reacted to the presence of the wind farm? Has it created jobs in the community? Has it increased the taxes collected by the community? Find out from the archives of local newspapers.

Investigate Different Turbines. Some turbines operate better at lower wind speeds, others at higher speeds. Which work better at your site: more small turbines or fewer large turbines?

Community Support. Was the entire local community supportive of the wind farm? What arguments were brought forth, both for and against? Were changes made to the plans to satisfy the opponents? Read reports from the wind farm developer, local action groups, and local newspapers.

Make an oral presentation to your classmates, who will act as local residents at a town meeting. Answer any questions they may have. Act as if this were a report on a proposed wind farm (not an existing one). Ask them to vote on whether to accept your project.

Where to Find Windmills

To understand the old European windmills, you should see the mighty sails turn and the giant gears mesh. You should watch the heavy millstones grind, and climb to the upstairs to feel the whole mill vibrate from the force of the wind as the sails flash by the window.

To know a North American windmill, you should hear the rattle of the wind in the vanes and the clatter of the pump as it raises water from deep in the earth.

To appreciate a modern wind turbine, you should stand beneath one to feel the wind rush through your hair and hear the deep whirring as the powerful blades turn in the wind.

Here's a list of various types of windmills that are open to the public in the United States, Canada, England, and the Netherlands.

European-Style Windmills

United States

CALIFORNIA

San Francisco
Golden Gate Park
www.sfwindmills.org/index.html
Two tower mills built in 1902 and 1905 pumped water to irrigate the sand dunes that became the lush gardens of Golden Gate Park. Video on website.

ILLINOIS

Geneva
Fabyan Windmill, Fabyan Forest Preserve
www.illinoiswindmills.org/index_files/Fabyan.htm
Working Dutch smock mill. Open seasonally.

Golden
Prairie Windmill
www.goldenwindmill.org
Working smock mill in the northern German style. Museum tells the history of the mill.

Fulton
De Immigrant Mill and Windmill Cultural Center
www.illinoiswindmills.org/index_files/Deimmigrant.htm
Built in the Netherlands in 2001, assembled in Fulton. Cultural Center contains scale models of European windmills.

Peotone
Rathje Windmill
www.illinoiswindmills.org/index_files/Peotone.htm
Smock mill open and awaiting restoration by the local historical society. Annual Old Mill Fall Festival held in September.

IOWA

Elk Horn

www.danishwindmill.com/danish_windmill_history/history_overview.asp
Working 1848 windmill brought from Denmark and restored in the 1970s. Museum and mill open year-round.

KANSAS

Hillsboro

www.hillsboro-museums.com/Friesenpage.html
Mennonite Settlement Museum contains an original farm and village with a reconstructed Dutch-style grist mill. Open May through October.

Smith Center

Old Dutch Mill, Wagner Park
www.smithcenterks.com
Open year-round.

Wamego

Schonhoff Windmill, Wamego Park
www.wamegohistoricalmuseum.org/dutchmill.html
Museum and mill, open year-round.

MARYLAND

Cambridge

Spocott Windmill
http://spocottwindmill.org
Restored postmill and 19th-century village. Open year-round.

MASSACHUSETTS

Cape Cod has the largest collection of restored European windmills in the United States. Most are open spring through fall and by appointment in the winter.

Brewster

Old Higgins Farm Windmill, Drummer Boy Park
www.brewsterhistoricalsociety.org/index.html
Working smock mill.

Chatham

Chatham Windmill, Chase Park
http://capecodwindmills.scificincinnati.com/chatham_windmill.htm
Open seasonally.

Eastham

Eastham Windmill, Windmill Park
www.easthamhistorical.org/b.html#Eastham%20Windmill
Built in 1680, it is the oldest and last working windmill on Cape Cod. Eastham Windmill Weekend held annually.

Nantucket

Nantucket Windmill
http://capecodwindmills.scificincinnati.com/nantucket_windmill.htm
Working mill grinds flour in summer.

Orleans

Jonathan Young Mill, Town Cove Park
www.orleanshistoricalsociety.org/JYW-01.html
All of the original machinery and parts are intact and operational in summer.

Sandwich

Old East Windmill, Heritage Museums and Gardens
http://heritagemuseumsandgardens.org/exhibitions/current-exhibitions/old-east-windmill/
A smock mill is one of the historical exhibits of the Heritage Museum and Gardens.

Yarmouth
Judah Baker Mill
www.hsoy.org/historic/judahbaker.htm
(508) 382-2231 ext. 237
Open seasonally.

MICHIGAN

Dearborn
Old Yarmouth Windmill, Greenfield Village
www.thehenryford.org/village/index.aspx
A Cape Cod windmill that was moved to Greenfield Village.

Holland
De Zwaan Windmill, Windmill Island
www.cityofholland.com/windmillislandgardens
Working windmill brought from the Netherlands and rebuilt on the island. Windmill Island is home to a historic Dutch village.

MINNESOTA

Mankato
Seppman Windmill, Minneopa State Park
http://en.wikipedia.org/wiki/Seppman_Mill
Partially restored windmill made of Sandstone. State Park open year-round.

NEW JERSEY

Milford
Volendam Windmill
www.co.hunterdon.nj.us/depts/c&h/huntmuseums.htm#windmill
Replica of a Dutch smock mill.

NEW YORK

Long Island has preserved many old windmills.

Bridgehampton
Beebe Windmill
http://en.wikipedia.org/wiki/Beebe_Windmill
(631) 537-1088
Tours during the summer.

East Hampton
East Hampton is home to three restored historic windmills. All are open to the public:

Gardiners Mill
http://easthampton.patch.com/listings/gardiner-mill
(631) 324-0713
Tours by appointment.

Hook Mill
www.easthampton.com/homesweethome/The_Windmills/Hook_Mill/hook_mill.html
Restored in 2005, open June through September, located on North Main Street.

Pantigo Mill, Home Sweet Home Museum
http://easthampton.patch.com/listings/pantigo-mill
Museum and windmill open year-round.

Water Mill
James Corwith Windmill
www.waymarking.com/waymarks/WMAE7D_Water_Mill_Water_Mill_NY
The smallest surviving grist mill on Long Island, located on the village green. The town also has a historic water mill and museum.

NORTH CAROLINA

Roanoke Island
Island Farm
www.currituckbeachlight.com/islandfarm/index.php
Living history farm interprets daily life on Roanoke Island in the mid-1800s. This working farm is restoring a 19th-century windmill. Open April through November.

RHODE ISLAND

Jamestown

Jamestown Windmill, Windmill Hill Historic District
www.jamestownhistoricalsociety.org/index.cfm?id=5
Restored smock windmill is part of the Windmill Hill historic district, which includes colonial buildings and the Quaker Meeting House. Open for tours on weekends July through September. Windmill Day is held every other year.

Middletown

Boyd's Mill, Paradise Park
www.middletownhistory.org/pages/boyds_mill.htm
Unique working windmill with eight sails. Open for tours Sundays only, May through September.

Middletown

Robert Sherman Windmill, Prescott Farm
www.newportrestoration.org/visit/prescott_farm/history_architecture #robert_sherman_windmill
Restored colonial era farm and grounds include unique smock mill with double grinding stones from 1812. Farm open year-round, workshops and tours in summer and fall.

SOUTH DAKOTA

Milbank

Milbank Grist Mill
www.milbanksd.com/visitor/attractions.php
Working restored smock mill and museum. Tours and demonstrations several times a year.

TEXAS

Lubbock

Flowerdew Hundred Postmill
www.windmill.com/flowerdew.html
Working replica of the first windmill built in America in 1621. Located at the American Wind Power Center and Museum.

Victoria

Victoria Grist Windmill, Memorial Park
www.waymarking.com/waymarks/WM1GBC
Restored smock mill.

VIRGINIA

Williamsburg

Robertsons Windmill, Colonial Williamsburg
www.history.org/almanack/life/trades/trademil.cfm
Working replica postmill located in Colonial Williamsburg. Open year-round.

Canada

MANITOBA

Steinbach

Mennonite Heritage Village Windmill
www.mennoniteheritagevillage.com/
Working replica Dutch smock mill is part of the Mennonite Heritage Village. Open year-round.

ONTARIO

Bayfield

Folmar Windmill
www.bayfield-on.worldweb.com/SightsAttractions/Specialty Attractions/
Working windmill that operates as a sawmill and grinds grain. Open June through August.

QUEBEC

Early French settlers built stone tower windmills in New France. The remains of 21 mills can be seen along the St. Lawrence River from Quebec City north to Riviere-Trios-Pistoles. The two listed below are restored and open to the public.

Montreal
Fleming Windmill, La Salle
www.montreal-travelguide.com/Pole-des-Rapides/Moulin
-Fleming-Lasalle/
Working mill is open in summer. Free tours every weekend; theatrical skits present the history of the mill.

St.-Louis-de-Ille-aux-Coudres
www.lesmoulinsiac.com/pages/historical.html
Working stone wind and water mill with museum, guided tours, seasonal activities, and a bakery. Open May through October.

The Netherlands

There are over 1,000 working windmills in Holland. For information and photographs, see www.windmillworld.com/europe/netherlands.htm.

North American Windmills

You can see thousands of old windmills on private farms and ranches throughout the midwestern and western United States. Some are still pumping water; others are not in working order. The following North American windmills are open to visitors.

United States

ILLINOIS

Batavia
Fox River Walk
www.bataviaparks.org/park27.htm
Many windmills are located on the river walk, all built in six local factories. Factory buildings can still be seen on the walk. The Railroad Depot Museum contains miniature windmills that salesmen used as samples.

INDIANA

Kendallville
Mid-American Windmill Museum
http://midamericawindmillmuseum.org
The museum has 52 windmills, including examples of all windmills built at Kendallville's Flint and Walling Company. Open April through November.

IOWA

Audubon
Nathaniel Hamlin Park
www.auduboncounty.net/achs1/park.html
Contains former farm and farm museum with 18 antique windmills. Open weekends, summer only.

Oscaloosa
Nelson Pioneer Farm Museum
www.nelsonpioneer.org
Pioneer farm and museum with working windmill along with other village buildings. Open May through October.

Urbandale
Living History Farms
www.lhf.org
Replicas of Native North American farming settlement, 1859 pioneer farm, 1900 farm, and 1875 village. The 1900 farm has a windmill. Open May through October.

KANSAS

Colby
Prairie Museum of Art and History
www.prairiemuseum.org/Home.html
Museum includes restored sod house settlement and 1930s farmhouse with an early wooden-blade windmill.

Wichita
Old Cowtown Museum
www.oldcowtown.org
Living history museum recreates a midwestern cattle town from the 1870s. Windmill stands near railroad depot.

MARYLAND

Oxon Hill
Oxon Hill Farm, Oxon Cove Park
www.nps.gov/oxhi/index.htm
Working living history farm with North American windmill. Part of the National Park Service, open year-round; free admission.

NEBRASKA

Grand Island
Stuhr Museum of the Prairie Pioneer
www.stuhrmuseum.org
Reconstructed railroad town with museum, farm, and two windmills. Open year-round.

Grand Island
Windmill State Recreation Area
http://visit.nebraska.gov/component/myplanner/detail/recreation/2000228
(308) 468-5700
A display of antique windmills at this lakeside campground.

Minden
Pioneer America Museum
www.pioneervillage.org/
Reconstructed pioneer village with 28 buildings, over 50,000 historical artifacts, and an old North American windmill. Open year-round.

Nebraska City
Kregel Windmill Museum
http://kregelwindmillfactorymuseum.org/about.htm
Old factory is now a museum; visit by appointment only. Admission is free and open to adults 18 years old and older.

OKLAHOMA

Shattuck
Shattuck Windmill Museum and Park
www.shattuckok.com/WindmillPark.html
Junction of highways 283 and 15.
The park has 37 windmills of various shapes and sizes. Open year-round.

TEXAS

Lubbock
American Wind Power Center and Museum
www.windmill.com/index.html
(806) 747-8734
An extensive collection of North American windmills, as well as large and small wind turbines. A mural 34 feet tall and 172 feet long tells the story of the past, present, and future of the windmill. Holds weekend introductory courses on careers in wind energy for students 18 years old and older. Open year-round.

WISCONSIN

Cassville
Stonefield Historic Site
http://stonefield.wisconsinhistory.org/
Living history site comprising an agricultural museum, 1901 farmstead, farming village, and windmill. Open June through October.

Canada

ALBERTA

Etzikom
Etzikom Museum and Canadian Historical Windpower Centre
www.facebook.com/etzikommuseum?sk=info
Museum of southeast Alberta, interpretive center, and 18 restored windmills, including a European postmill. Open summer only.

Wind Turbines

Most wind farms are located on private land. Do not enter the land without permission from the owner. Many wind turbines can be seen from public roads.

United States

A list of large wind farms in the United States is found at http://en.wikipedia.org/wiki/List_of_wind_farms_in_the_United_States. Your state energy commission may contain a list of wind farms as well. Some wind farms may offer tours.

Tehachapi
The Tehachapi-Mojave Wind Resource Area in Tehachapi, California
www.wind-works.org/articles/TehachapiTourGuide.html
The Pacific Crest Trail runs through this area. You can hike for several miles among some of the 5,000 wind turbines. Tour map at the above website.

Canada

Most wind farms are located on private land. Do not enter the land without permission from the owner. Many wind turbines can be seen from public roads. A list of large wind farms in Canada is found at http://en.wikipedia.org/wiki/List_of_wind_farms_in_Canada.

Europe

Maps and lists of wind farms in Europe can be found at www.thewindpower.net/wind_farms_europe.php.

Australia

A list of large wind farms in Australia can be found at http://en.wikipedia.org/wiki/List_of_wind_farms_in_Australia.

Resources

RENEWABLE ENERGY AND WIND ENERGY GROUPS

American Wind Energy Association (AWEA)
www.awea.org
Presents news, information, and reports on wind energy in the United States.

Canadian Wind Energy Association (CanWEA)
www.canwea.ca
The wind energy industry in Canada.

European Wind Energy Association
www.ewea.org
Fact sheets and reports give information about the wind industry in different countries in Europe (www.ewea.org/index.php?id=1922); interactive display about how a wind turbine works, both on land and offshore.

Global Wind Energy Council
www.gwec.net
Information about wind energy around the world.

Kidwind
http://learn.kidwind.org
Wind-related curriculum materials and projects, including a design contest to build your own turbine.

National Renewable Energy Laboratory (NREL)
www.nrel.gov/learning/re_wind.html
Learning About Wind Energy page includes links to more information about renewable energy.

US Department of Energy: Energy Efficiency and Renewable Energy
www.windpoweringamerica.gov
Maps, latest news, databases, and more.

US Energy Information Administration: Energy Kids
www.eia.gov/kids
Presents renewable and nonrenewable energy sources, including wind.

Women of Wind Energy
www.womenofwindenergy.org
Promotes the professional development of women in the wind energy industry.

STUDENT ENVIRONMENTAL GROUPS

There are hundreds of environmental programs that include children. The websites below describe a few of them and link you to many more.

Global Wind Day
www.globalwindday.org
Describes celebration events all around the world.

National Audubon Society
http://education.audubon.org
The Audubon website has a whole section for kids, which presents games, school projects, and more (http://policy.audubon.org/climate-change -campaign). Good information on the effects of climate change.

National Resources Defense Council
www.nrdc.org/reference/kids.asp
Links to dozens of other environmental groups for kids.

Roots and Shoots
www.rootsandshoots.org
Local groups that work on environmental programs of their choice. Founded by Jane Goodall.

Sierra Club
www.sierraclub.org/education/newsletter/
Concerned with wildlife preservation and a healthy environment. The Sierra Club has a newsletter for children available online.

US Environmental Protection Agency: Calculate Greenhouse Gas Emissions
www.epa.gov/climatechange/emissions/ind_calculator.html
Complete the survey to learn about your environmental footprint and how to reduce it.

HISTORICAL ASSOCIATIONS

International Windmillers' Association
Dr. T. Lindsay Baker
PO Box 507
Rio Vista, TX 76093
Holds an annual trade fair with demonstrations of windmill restoration and tours of windmill collections. Publishers of Windmillers' Gazette: A Journal for the Preservation of America's Wind Power History and Heritage *(www.windmillersgazette.com).*

National Register of Historic Places
www.nps.gov/nr/
Search their database for windmills.

Windmill World
www.windmillworld.com/
Website includes locations of many historic windmills and watermills around the world, windmill history, and other links.

Windmill Careers

Do you like working outdoors in all kinds of weather? Or fiddling with machines? Do you want to invent a better wind turbine? Or take charge of a bank of computers that tracks the electricity generated by a wind farm? Or study the geology and wildlife of a windy landscape? Or talk to people about building a wind farm in their community? A vast range of jobs is open to men and women in the fast-growing wind energy industry.

Engineers and technicians of all sorts form part of the team that designs the technology of the present and future. They include

> ❯ aerospace engineers
>
> ❯ civil engineers
>
> ❯ electrical engineers
>
> ❯ environmental engineers
>
> ❯ industrial engineers
>
> ❯ material engineers
>
> ❯ mechanical engineers

Scientists play a role in the wind power industry as well; they study a site for a wind farm and monitor it after the turbines are erected.

They include

> ❯ atmospheric scientists, or meteorologists
>
> ❯ wildlife biologists
>
> ❯ geologists
>
> ❯ environmental scientists

These engineering and science jobs require a college degree, and often a graduate degree as well.

Skilled workers are also needed to manufacture turbine components and construct wind farms, such as

> ❯ machinists
>
> ❯ computer-controlled machine tool operators
>
> ❯ welders
>
> ❯ inspectors and production managers
>
> ❯ construction equipment operators
>
> ❯ electricians

Training for these careers ranges from apprenticeship programs, to vocational school courses, to on-the-job experience.

Once the wind turbines are erected, wind technicians enter the picture. These are the men and women who climb the towers and work inside the **nacelle**—the body of the turbine on top of the tower—to perform routine maintenance and repair the turbines. Community colleges and technical schools offer one- and two-year programs in wind technology training. Some of these programs include hands-on training with turbines.

In addition, the industry needs businesspeople of all sorts to handle real estate matters, legal and zoning issues, finances, community relations, and much more. Whatever your talents and interests, the booming wind energy field may have a place for you.

For more information on colleges, universities, and institutes that offer wind technology courses, visit www.windustry.org/where-can-i -find-a-school-or-training-program-specific-to-renewable-energy.

For detailed descriptions of jobs in the wind energy field, visit www .bls.gov/green/wind_energy/wind_energy.pdf.

Glossary

Aermotor windmill: a windmill first developed in the 1800s by Thomas Perry, who conducted more than 5,000 experiments to arrive at this model

axis: on a windmill, a shaft around which windmill blades rotate (see also **vertical axis windmill** and **horizontal axis windmill**)

bellows: a pump that blows air through a tube; used to blow air on a fire to make it burn hotter

cracks: lines cut on a millstone to make the grain grind evenly

dhow: an ancient sailing boat

dike: a wall, usually made of earth, built to hold back water

drainage windmill: windmill that lifts water from one level to another; used to drain lowlands in England and the Netherlands; also used to regulate water levels for flood control and irrigation

Eclipse windmill: first designed in the 1850s by Leonard Wheeler, a windmill with a small side wind vane that, in a strong wind, turns the windmill wheel sideways

fantail: a round fan of small wind vanes mounted on the back of a windmill that automatically moves the large sail to face directly into the wind

fen: a lowland covered partly or wholly with water

fossil fuel: a nonrenewable energy source such as coal, petroleum, or natural gas, which derives from fossils that are millions of years old and is burned to generate power

fulling mill: a windmill used to pound woolen cloth into felt; called stink mills by the Dutch because rancid butter and urine were used in the processing of this material

global warming: a steady increase in average temperatures throughout the world caused by an increase in carbon dioxide and other gases building up in the atmosphere and attributed to burning fossil fuels and other industrial processes

glue mill: a windmill that processes animal hide and bones to make glue

grist mill: a mill for grinding grain

guild: in the Middle Ages, a group of men working in the same trade or craft

Halladay windmill: a windmill design that included tilting wind vanes so the wind blew through them when the wind grew too strong

horizontal axis windmill: a windmill in which blades or sails are attached to a horizontal axis or support and rotate vertically, such as a postmill, smock mill, or contemporary propeller-type wind turbine

hulling mill: a mill that extracts the outer layer of rice and barley kernels

Jacobs wind plant: a small windmill, designed by Marcellus Jacobs, that could generate 400 to 500 kilowatt-hours of electricity per month; popular among farmers in isolated areas in the early 20th century

kilowatt: equal to 1,000 watts

kilowatt-hour (kWh): a unit of energy that uses one kilowatt (1,000 watts) in one hour; unit of measurement for home electricity use

mathematical windmill: name given to the windmill designed by Thomas Perry and other inventors who used scientific experiments and mathematical formulas to build stronger and more efficient machines

megawatt: one million watts; used to measure power output by individual wind turbines

millstone: large, circular stone used in a windmill to grind or crush grain or other materials

millwright: a person who designs and builds windmills, sets up machinery, and repairs windmill machinery

nacelle: body of a propeller-type modern wind turbine

nonrenewable energy: energy from a source that is not easily replaced, such as fossil fuels or nuclear energy

North American windmill: a design incorporating many thin blades that turn in the wind and that raise water using an underground pump; first developed in the American West and now used worldwide

oil mill: a windmill that presses oil from seeds

paint mill: a windmill that grinds pigments for paint

patent sail: a windmill sail with wooden slats like window shutters; weights inside a mill could adjust the speed of the sails by opening and closing these shutters as the wind speed changed

polder: flatland in the Netherlands that has been reclaimed from the sea and is protected by dikes

postmill: a windmill supported by a single sturdy post with four sails revolving around it in the direction of the wind; when the wind direction changed, millers had to change the direction of the sails to face them into the wind; first seen in Europe around 1200

reef: to reduce the size of a canvas sail by rolling and tying it up with ropes

renewable energy: energy from a source that is easily replaced, such as wind power, solar power, water power, and biomass (plant products)

rotor: the rotating part of a windmill, including the blades and blade assembly

rudder: a wooden or metal plate behind the vanes of a North American windmill that controls the direction of the vanes

sawmill: a windmill that saws logs into lumber

sawyer: a person who works in a sawmill

slodger: nickname for a person who lived in the fens or marshlands of eastern England and who fought against the windmills that were built to drain the marshes

Smith-Putnam wind turbine: huge, experimental wind turbine built in Vermont, developed by Palmer Putnam, and in operation from 1941 to 1943

smock mill: a windmill created in the 1300s that had sails attached to the roof or cap of the mill that revolved on an outdoor track; when wind direction changed, only the sails needed to be adjusted to face into the wind; bigger, heavier, and stronger mills than the earlier postmill design

squall: a sudden, violent wind often accompanied by rain or snow

stone dresser: traveling craftsman who sharpened millstones

terawatt: one billion watts; used to measure the energy production of wind turbines

tower windmill: a round stone tower with windmill sails that was common in Mediterranean countries

turn wheel: a wheel located outside a mill that allows a miller to turn the sails by hand

vertical axis windmill: windmill design with blades, attached to a vertical axis or support, that rotate horizontally; includes ancient Persian windmills and modern experimental windmills

watt: a unit of power used to measure electrical current

wind: movement of air caused by the uneven heating of the earth by the sun; air movement caused when warm air expands and rises and is replaced by cool air

wind farm: group of wind turbines clustered together; often owned and maintained by one energy development company

wind turbine: name commonly used to refer to wind-powered machines that generate electricity

wind vane: a device that rotates to show the direction of the wind

windmill: a machine operated by the wind with sails or vanes that drive machinery to grind, pump, or perform other mechanical tasks

windmill sail: the wooden arms of a European-style windmill; also the canvas sheets that cover the wooden sails

windmiller: a person who traveled from ranch to ranch installing and repairing self-operating North American windmills; a person who operates a European-style windmill that grinds grain, pumps water, and more

windsmith: a person who inspects and repairs modern wind turbines

Picture Key
to Windmills

Paint mill

Drainage windmill

Grist mill

North American windmill

Postmill

Smith-Putnam wind turbine

Smock mill

Tower windmill

Vertical Axis Wind Turbine

Wind Turbines

Bibliography

WEBSITES

Community Wind Development Handbook
www.auri.org/wp-content/assets/legacy/research/Community%20
Wind%20Handbook.pdf
Want to start a community wind project? Read on.

Grist: How to Talk to a Climate Skeptic
www.grist.org/article/series/skeptics
Answers to questions about scientific evidence for climate change.

KidWind Project: Wind Energy History
http://learn.kidwind.org/learn/wind_basics_history
Presents the basics of wind power.

National Geographic: Harness the Power of Wind
http://environment.nationalgeographic.com/environment/global
-warming/wind-power-interactive.html
Create your own wind farm on this interactive website.

US Department of Energy: Energy Basics
www.eere.energy.gov/basics/renewable_energy/wind_turbines.html
Basic description of how wind turbines work.

US Department of Energy: Wind Energy Myths
www.nrel.gov/docs/fy05osti/37657.pdf
A government fact sheet that examines arguments against wind power.

US Department of Energy: Wind Powering America
www.windpoweringamerica.gov/schools/
Wind for Schools Project with links to project locations, educational programs, and more.

What's Inside a Wind Turbine?
www.youtube.com/watch?v=LNXTm7aHvWc
An animated video showing what's inside a wind turbine.

Where Does Wind Power Come From? Climbing Inside a Wind Turbine
www.youtube.com/watch?v=x8PjVoYRuYs
Video showing what it's like to climb a wind turbine.

World Meteorological Organization: Did You Ever Wonder . . .
www.wmo.int/youth/index_en.html
World Meteorological Organization discusses climate, climate change, experiments, and how to become a meteorologist.

BOOKS

Titles preceded by an asterisk are written for an adult audience.

*Baker, T. Lindsay. *Field Guide to American Windmills*. Norman, OK: University of Oklahoma Press, 1985.
*Brangwyn, Frank, and Hayter Preston. *Windmills*. London: John Lane, The Bodley Head Ltd., 1923.
*Brooks, Laura. *Windmills*. New York: Metro Books, 1999.

Cherry, Lynne, and Braasch, Gary. *How We Know What We Know About Our Changing Climate: Scientists and Kids Explore Global Warming.* Nevada City, CA: Dawn Publications, 2008.

Delano, Marfé Ferguson. *Earth in the Hot Spot: Bulletins from a Warming World.* Washington, DC: National Geographic, 2009.

Drummond, Alan. *Energy Island: How One Community Harnessed the Wind and Changed Their World.* New York: Farrar, Straus and Giroux, 2011.

*Gipe, Paul. *Wind Energy Basics: A Guide to Home- and Community-Scale Wind-Energy Systems.* White River Junction, VT: Chelsea Green Publishing, 2009.

*Hefner, Robert. *Windmills of Long Island.* New York: Society for the Preservation of Long Island Antiquities and W. W. Norton & Company, 1983.

Kamkwamba, William, and Mealer, Bryan. *The Boy Who Harnessed the Wind.* New York: William Morrow, 2009.

*Lombardo, Daniel. *Windmills of New England.* Cape Cod, MA: On Cape Publications, 2003.

Ride, Sally, and Tam O'Shaughnessy. *Mission: Planet Earth; Our World and Its Climate—and How Humans Are Changing Them.* New York: Roaring Brook, 2009.

*Singer, Charles, E. J. Holmyard, A. R. Hall, and Trevor Williams, ed. *A History of Technology.* Vols. 2, 3, and 4. Oxford: Clarendon Press, 1954.

*Skilton, C. P. *British Windmills and Watermills.* London: Collins, 1947.

Spier, Peter. *Of Dikes and Windmills.* Garden City, NY: Doubleday, 1969.

*Wailes, Rex. *The English Windmill.* London: Routledge & Kegan Paul Ltd., 1954.

*Watts, Martin. *Windmills.* Princes Risborough, England: Shire Publications, 2006

Woodward, John. *Eyewitness: Climate Change.* London: DK Publishing, 2008.

AUTHOR INTERVIEWS

Paul Gipe, author and renewable energy industry analyst, August 2, 2011.
Dan Juhl, CEO, Juhl Wind, Inc., September 2, 2011.
Richard Miller, operations manager, Hull (MA) Municipal Light Plant, August 16, 2011.
Michael Wheeler, Director, Project Finance, enXco, June 15, 2011.

SOURCE NOTES

1. Harnessing Wind Power Through Time
Sources include *Of Dikes and Windmills*, by Peter Spier; www.awea.org/learnabout/publications/upload/20percent_Wind_factsheet.pdf.

2. Ancient Wind Machines
Sources include *A History of Technology*, vol. 2, edited by Charles Singer, E. J. Holmyard, A. R. Hall, and Trevor Williams; for Gill Juleff's research: http://sundaytimes.lk/080831/Plus/sundaytimesplus_09.html.

3. Windmills in Europe Across the Centuries
Sources include *Past and Present*, book 2, chapter 15, by Thomas Carlyle; *The English Windmill*, by Rex Wailes; *British Windmills and Watermills*, by C. P. Skilton; *Windmills*, by Martin Watts; *Of Dikes and Windmills*, by Peter Spier; *A History of Technology*, vols. 2, 3, and 4, edited by Charles Singer, E. J. Holmyard, A. R. Hall, and Trevor Williams; and author interviews and research in the Netherlands.

4. A Windmiller's Life
Sources include *Of Dikes and Windmills*, by Peter Spier; *The English Windmill*, by Rex Wailes; *British Windmills and Watermills*, by C. P. Skilton; and author interviews and research in the Netherlands.

5. All-American Windmills
Sources include *Windmills of New England*, by David Lombardo; *Field Guide to American Windmills*, by T. Lindsay Baker; and personal interviews.

6. Inventors and Cowboys Work the Wind
Sources include *Field Guide to American Windmills*, by T. Lindsay Baker; and personal research and interviews.

7. A New Kind of Windmill
Sources include *Field Guide to American Windmills*, by T. Lindsay Baker; *A History of Technology*, vol. 4, edited by Charles Singer, E. J. Holmyard, A. R. Hall, and Trevor Williams; and interviews.

8. Wind Power Today
European wind generation 2010: http://blog.ewea.org/2011/07/wind-industry-consistently-blowing-stronger-than-expected; European wind generation 2010–2050: www.ewea.org/fileadmin/ewea_documents/documents/publications/reports/Pure_Power_III.pdf; US wind generation 2010: www.awea.org/learnabout/publications/factsheets/upload/2010-Annual-Market-Report-Rankings-Fact-Sheet-May-2011.pdf; US wind power 20 percent by 2030: www.20percentwind.org/20percent_wind_energy_report_revOct08.pdf (DOE full report), www.20percentwind.org/20p_Wind_Flier.pdf (fact sheet); Tehachapi, California, project: http://energybible.com/wind_energy/tehacnapi_wind_farm.html.

9. A Solution in the Wind
IPCC report conclusions: www.grist.org/article/series/skeptics; wind energy key to climate change solution: www.gwec.net/index.php?id=151; health costs of coal: www.lungusa.org/about-us/our-impact/top-stories/ending-free-pass-polluters.html; mountaintop coal mining: www.sierraclub.org/coal/mtr/; protecting birds and bats: www.awea.org/learnabout/publications/upload/Wind-Energy-and-Wildlife_May-2011.pdf, www.gwec.net/index.php?id=144&L=0; Audubon Society position on wind power: http://policy.audubon.org/wind-power-overview-0; study of offshore wind farms: www.gwec.net/index.php?id=145&L=0; study of sound of turbines (executive summary): www.awea.org/issues/siting/upload/Executive_Summary_AWEA_and_CanWEA_Sound_White_Paper.pdf; opponents to telephone poles: "The War on Telephone Poles" by Eula Biss, *Harper's Magazine*, February 2009.

10. Fulfilling the Promise
Turbines on leased farm and ranch land: www.powerofwind.com/documents/AmericanWindpowerBrochure.pdf; income to local communities: www.20percentwind.org/20p_Wind_Flier.pdf; wind for schools: www.windpoweringamerica.gov/schools_wfs_project.asp; Hull, Massachusetts, wind project: www.hullwind.org; community-based wind: www.auri.org/research/Community%20Wind%20Handbook.pdf, www.juhlwind.com/communitywind.html, www.cascadecommunitywind.com; additional information was gathered in author interviews with Paul Gipe, Dan Juhl, Richard Miller, and Michael Wheeler.

Index

A

activities
  airflow and temperature, 8–9
  apple-cranberry cobbler, 47
  conservation of electricity, 90–91
  corn dodgers, 61
  day without electricity, 73
  electricity usage, 70–71
  element temperatures, 6–7
  environmental action, 103
  Global Wind Day, 112
  investigating a wind farm, 113
  landscape art, 37
  life before electricity, 72
  local energy sources, 102
  measuring the wind, 16–17
  milling grain, 25
  on-the-trail beans, 62
  paper collage, 48–49
  pillow cover, 52–53
  pot holder, 50–51
  reading electric bills and meter, 86–89
  sing a song, 63
  whole wheat rolls, 38–39
  wind sock and wind vane, 14–15
  writing about the wind, 26–27
Aermotor Company, 56, 57
Aermotor windmills, 56–57, 127
airflow and temperature (activity), 8–9
Alphonse Daudet's Windmill in Fontvieille (Van Gogh painting), 36
Altamont Pass, CA, 97–98
America. *See* United States
American West, 42, 45, 58–60, 67
American Wind Energy Association (AWEA), 99, 123
Antarctica, 67
Antelope Valley, CA, 111
Appalachia, 96
apple-cranberry cobbler (activity), 47
Arctic Ocean, 65–66
Audubon Society, 98, 124
axis, 13, 127. *See also* vertical axis windmills

B

Barbour, Erwin, 44
Batavia, IL, 43, 60
Battle-Ax windmills, 45
beans, on-the-trail (activity), 62
Beaufort, Francis, 16
Beaufort scale, 16–17
bed stone, 3
Bell, Alexander Graham, 100
bellows, 12, 127
birds, protection of, 97–98
blades
  turbine, 4, 68, 76–77, 83, 98
  wood versus steel, 55–56, 66
  See also sails
brake mechanisms, 3, 30, 32
bread, 25, 31, 38, 61
Breukelen (Brooklyn), NY, 42
Brush, Charles, 67
Bryant, John, 32
bucks, 20
Burnham, John, 42, 43
Byrd, Richard, 67

C

California
  salt works in, 46
  wind farms in, 5, 84–85, 97–98, 111
California Institute of Technology, 111
Campo de Critana, La Mancha, Spain, 21

Canadian Wind Energy Association (CanWEA), 99, 123
Cape Cod, 43, 116
carbon dioxide, 94, 101
careers in wind technology, 125–126
Carr, Tom, 105
Catholics, in Protestant Reformation, 35–36
Cherry County, NE, 45
China
    kites in, 11
    wind power in, 4, 75, 76, 80
    windmills in, 13
climate change/global warming, 5, 31, 93–95, 98, 109, 110, 127
coal, 68, 93–94
    health costs of, 95–96
    tax incentives for, 83
cobbler, apple-cranberry (activity), 47
cogwheels, 3
collage, paper (activity), 48–49
Columbian Exposition, 57
community-owned wind farms, 108–110
corn bread, 61
corn dodgers (activity), 61
cowboy songs, 62, 63
"Cowboy's Gettin'-Up Holler" (song), 62
cracks (millstone feature), 33, 127
Crusaders, 20
Cubitt, William, 24

D

Danish Wind Electricity Company, 65
deafness, among millers, 32

decoration of windmills, 35
Deepwater Horizon, 97
Denmark, 22, 65, 66, 108
Deptford, England, 23
dhows, 11, 127
dikes, 1, 21, 22, 127
DOE (US Department of Energy), 80, 106, 107, 108, 123
drainage windmills, 21, 30, 127, 130
dressing millstones, 33
droughts, 44–45, 93–94
Dutch Resistance, 36

E

Eclipse windmills, 43, 44, 46, 127
efficiency
    of electricity usage, 91
    of wind turbines, 77
    of windmills, 43, 44, 55–56
Egypt, 11, 13
electrical power
    Benjamin Franklin and, 11–12
    conservation of (activity), 90–91
    life before/without (activities), 72–73
    reading electric bills and meter (activity), 86–89
    units of measurement for, 85
    usage of, (activity), 70–71
    wind power and, 75
    windmills and, 65–69
element temperatures (activity), 6–7
emissions, greenhouse gas, 80, 88, 95
energy conservation, 90–91, 95

England
Dean Herbert's windmill in, 19
draining fens in, 21–22
fantail invention in, 23–24
offshore wind farms in, 79
sawyers in, 23
environmental action (activity), 103
environmental concerns, 93, 96–99
environmental groups, 103, 123–124
EPA (US Environmental Protection Agency), 95, 124
Europe
offshore wind farms in, 76
wind turbines in, 75, 76
windmillers in, 29–36
windmills in, 19–24, 36
See also specific countries in Europe
European Commission, 80
European Wind Energy Association, 123

F

factory-made windmills, 42–44
fantails, 23–24, 127
farms
and windmills, 44–45
and wind turbines, 105–106, 110
See also wind farms
feed-in tariffs, 83, 84, 108
fens, 21–22, 127
fire hazards, 31
flour, 2, 19, 25, 33
fossil fuels, 5, 68, 93–96, 127

France, 22
Franklin, Benjamin, 11–12
fulling mills, 22, 127
furnaces, 12
furrows (millstone feature), 33

G

galvanization, 56–57
generators, 4, 66, 67, 83. *See also* wind turbines
Genghis Khan, 13
Germany, 22, 108
invasion of Netherlands, 36
Gipe, Paul, 99
global warming/climate change, 5, 31, 93–95, 98, 109, 110, 127
Global Wind Day, 123
celebrate (activity), 112
Global Wind Energy Council, 123
glue mills, 22, 127
gold miners, 46
grain, 2, 20, 31, 33, 129
chutes, 3
milling (activity), 25
mills, 34 (*see also* grist mills)
Grand Island, NE, 45
Grandpa's Knob, Rutland, VT, 68
Great American Desert, 42
Great Depression, 67
Great Plains, 43, 44–45, 58, 81
great spur wheels, 3
Greece, 21
greenhouse gases, 80, 88, 94, 95, 97, 101
grinding mills. *See* grist mills

grindstones. *See* millstones
grist mills, 3, 22, 30, 31, 127, 130
guilds, 23, 127
Gulf of Mexico, 97

H

Halladay, Daniel, 42–43, 55
Halladay windmills, 44, 55, 127
harps (millstone feature), 33
health hazards
    of coal power, 95
    of milling, 31–32
    of wind turbines, 99
Hemphill, Tim, 105
Herbert, Dean, 19
historical associations, 60, 124
Holland. *See* Netherlands
Homestead Act (1862), 63
hoppers, 3
horizontal axis windmills, 127
Hudson River Valley, 42
Hull, MA, 98, 107–108
Hull Municipal Light Plant, 107
hulling mills, 22, 127
humor, millers', 34–35
hydropower projects, 97

I

India, 76, 80
indoor plumbing, 60
Industrial Revolution, 24
inns, 30

Intergovernmental Panel on Climate Change
    (IPCC), 94
International Windmillers' Association, 124
inventors
    wind turbine, 76, 79, 106, 111
    windmill, 42–43, 55–56, 65–67

J

Jacobs, Joe, 66
Jacobs, Marcellus, 66, 69
Jacobs Wind Electric Company, 66
Jacobs wind plants, 66–67, 69, 127
Japan, 79, 80
Juhl, Dan, 108, 109
Juhl, Tyler, 110
Juhl Wind Company, 108–110
Juleff, Gill, 12

K

Kansas, 106
Kidwind, 123
kilowatt-hours (kWh), 66, 128
kilowatts (kW), 85, 128
Kinderdijk, Netherlands, 21
kites, 11–12

L

LaCour, Poul, 65–66
lands (millstone feature), 33
landscape art (activity), 37
Laramie, WY, 44

Lee, Edmund, 23
lightning bolts, 11–12, 32
local energy sources (activity), 102
Long Island, NY, 43

M

maintenance
    of wind turbines, 77, 79, 83, 106, 126
    of windmills, 32–33, 56, 59
mathematical windmills, 55–56, 128
measurement
    of electrical power, 85
    of wind speed, 16–17
Medlock, Frank O., 57
megawatts (MW), 79, 128
Meikle, Andrew, 24
messages, 35–36
methane, 97, 101
Mexico, 80
Mill at Work, The (Ruisdael painting), 4
Miller, Richard, 108
milling
    grain (activity), 25
    hazards of, 31–32
millstones, 2, 20, 31, 33, 128
millwrights, 20, 128. See also windmillers
mine shafts, 22, 45
Minnesota, 66, 79, 108–109

N

nacelles, 83, 126, 128
Nansen, Fridtjof, 65–66

National Audubon Society, 98, 124
National Register of Historic Places, 124
National Renewable Energy Laboratory
    (NREL), 106, 107, 123
National Resources Defense Council (NRDC),
    124
natural gas, 5, 83, 93–94
Nebraska, 45
Netherlands, 1, 21, 22, 24, 34, 35–36
New Amsterdam, 41, 42
New York City, 41–42
Newport, RI, 43
nonrenewable energy, 128. See also fossil fuels;
    nuclear power; renewable energy
North American windmills, 43, 57–58, 60,
    128, 130
North Dakota, 79, 94
North Pole, 65–66
Noyes, La Verne, 56
nuclear power, 68, 77
nursery rhymes, 31, 34

O

offshore wind farms, 76, 77, 79, 98, 108
oil, 5, 68, 83, 93–94
    spills, 96, 97
oil mills, 22, 32, 128

P

paint mills, 22, 32, 128, 130
paper mills, 23, 34
patchwork quilts, 48

patent sails, 24, 128
Perry, Thomas O., 55–56
Persia, 12–13
pillow cover (activity), 52–53
plumbing, indoor, 60
polders, 21, 22, 38, 128
pollution, 5, 94, 95–96
postmills, 20, 32, 128, 131
pot holder (activity), 50–51
propellers. *See* blades
Protestant Reformation, 35–36
pumps, 44–45
"put his nose to the grindstone,"
    origin of, 33
Putnam, Palmer, 67–68

Q

quilts, 48

R

races, skating, 31
radio, 66
railroads and windmills, 43–44
reefing, 30–31, 128
Rembrandt van Rijn, 2
renewable energy
    definition of, 128
    future of, 80
    government incentives for, 83
    rates, 83
    sources of, 96–97
    wind power as, 5

repairs. *See* maintenance
Rhode Island, 43
rolls, whole wheat (activity), 38–39
Roosevelt, Franklin, 67
Roots and Shoots, 124
rotors, 77, 128
rudders, 44, 128
Ruisdael, Jacob van, 4
"rule of thumb," origin of, 33
runner stones, 3
Rural Electrification Project, 67
rust prevention, 56–57
Rutland, VT, 68

S

sails, 1, 2, 129
    cloth, 24
    improvements to, 23–24
    patent, 24, 128
    reefing, 30–31
    wooden, 24, 30
    See also blades
salt works, 46
Samson (abbot), 19
sawmills, 23, 128
sawyers, 23, 128
schools, and wind turbines, 106
Scotland, 79
sea walls. *See* dikes
seal of New York City, 42
Sears Roebuck, 44
sharpening millstones, 33
"show your metal," origin of, 33

Sierra Club, 124
signaling, using windmills, 35–36
sing a song (activity), 63
skating races, 31
skirts (millstone feature), 33
slodgers, 21–22, 128
Smeaton, John, 24
smelting furnaces, 12
Smith-Putnam wind turbines, 68, 128, 131
smock mills, 20, 128, 131
solar power, 97
songs, cowboy, 62, 63
Souris River, 94
South Korea, 80
Southern California Edison (SCE), 84
Spain, 21
squalls, 32, 128. *See also* storms
Sri Lanka, 12
"Starving to Death on My Government Claim"
        (song), 63
steam engines, 4, 36
stink mills, 22
stitching (millstone feature), 33
stone dressers, 33, 128
storms, 22, 29, 30–31, 93. *See also* squalls
subsidies, energy, 83
sweep, steam-powered, 55

T

tariffs, 83, 84, 108
Tehachapi, CA, 84–85
Tehachapi Renewable Transmission Project
        (TRTP), 84–85

telephones, 100
temperatures
        element (activity), 6–7
        wind (activity), 8–9
terawatt hours (TWh), 85, 128
Texas, 79
tower windmills, 21, 128, 131
turbines. *See* wind turbines
turn wheels, 30, 128

U

Union Pacific Railroad, 43–44
United States
        future of wind power in, 80
        wind power capacity in, 75, 76, 82
        wind speeds in, 81
        windmills in, 41–46
        See also American West
US Department of Energy (DOE), 80, 106, 107,
        108, 123
US Energy Information Administration, 123
US Environmental Protection Agency (EPA),
        95, 124
US Weather Service, 12
US Wind Engine and Pump Company, 55–56,
        60

V

van Gogh, Vincent, 36
vehicles, hybrid electric, 95
vertical axis windmills, 13, 128,
        131

W

wallowers, 3

water mills, 2

Waterwolf, 1, 21

watts, 66, 85, 128

weather, 30, 32, 34, 93

Wheeler, Leonard R., 43

whole wheat rolls (activity), 38–39

wind

    definition of, 129

    measurement of (activity), 16–17

    writing about (activity), 26–27

wind currents, 2, 4, 81

wind farms, 77–80

    community-owned, 108–109

    definition of, 129

    investigating (activity), 113

    leasing arrangements for, 105

    offshore, 76, 77, 79, 98, 108

    opposition to, 99

    protection of birds and, 97–98

    scientific studies of, 98

    tax benefits from, 105–106

Wind for Schools Project, 106, 107, 133

wind furnaces, 12

wind plants, 66–67, 69, 127

wind power

    ancient sources of, 11–13

    benefits of, 80, 83, 110

    challenges to, 83

    cost of, 85, 110

    current capacity, in U.S., 75, 76, 82

    efficiency of, 77–78

    electricity and, 75

    employment opportunities and, 106

    future of, 80

    history of, 2–5

    in 21st century, 75–85

Wind Power Pioneer Award, 107–108

wind sock and wind vane (activity), 14–15

wind speed, 16–17, 81

wind tunnels, 13, 55

wind turbines

    arguments against, 99

    birds and, 97–98

    in the community, 107–110

    definition of, 129

    description of, 4–5

    efficiency of, 77–78

    in Europe, 75, 76

    health hazards of, 99

    image of, 131

    maintenance of, 77, 79, 83, 106, 126

    parts of, 83

    "payback time" of, 95

    production of, 106

    schools and, 106

    Smith-Putnam, 68, 128, 131

    in the United States, 75, 76, 82

    where to find, 121

    working with, 125–126

wind vanes, 15, 23, 43, 56, 83, 129

windmill paper collage (activity), 48–49

windmill sails. *See* sails

windmill towers, 59–60

Windmill World, 124

windmillers, 1, 20, 29–36, 58–59, 129

windmills
    in America, 41–46
    definition of, 129
    Dutch, 1
    electricity and, 65–69
    European, 19–24, 36
    factory-made, 42–44
    history of, 4
    homemade, 44–45
    industry of, 57
    maintenance of, 32–33, 56, 59
    naming of, 34
    opposition to, 23
    parts of, 3
    Persian, 12–13
    picture key to, 130–131
    scientific studies of, 55–57
    as signal devices, 35–36
    uses for, 22–23, 44, 45–46, 59–60
    where to find, 115–120
    wood versus steel, 56–57
    at the World's Columbian
        Exposition, 57
    See also specific types of windmills
windshafts, 3
windsmiths, 106, 129
Women of Wind Energy, 123
World War II, 36, 68
World's Columbian Exposition, 57
Wright, Wilbur and Orville, 12

X

XIT Ranch, 59

About the Author

Gretchen Woelfle is an award-winning author of picture books, short stories, and environmental nonfiction. She has written for *Cricket*, *Spider*, and *Cicada* magazines and the anthology series Stories from Where We Live.

978-1-55652-720-3
$14.95 (CAN $16.95)
Also available in e-book formats

Lighthouses for Kids
History, Science, and Lore with 21 Activities

KATHERINE L. HOUSE

What was it like to be a lighthouse keeper's kid, living in a remote, dangerous place far from stores, schools, or doctors? How did lighthouse lights shine so bright at a time when people had only candles and lamps? How do you build a sturdy lighthouse on top of soft, sandy soil—or on top of solid rock? Bringing to life an era when rivers, lakes, and oceans were the nation's highways and lighthouses served as traffic signals and maps, *Lighthouses for Kids* explores the history, science, and lore of lighthouses and provides firsthand stories of the challenges faced by lighthouse keepers and their families.

This comprehensive resource includes a field guide to US lighthouses, places to visit, a time line, glossary, websites to explore, a reading list for further study, and 21 creative and fun activities. Readers will learn to tie a bowline knot, build a model lighthouse, investigate how lighthouses flashed long ago, create a lighthouse logbook, witness the power of hydraulics, and much more.

Available at your favorite bookstore, by calling
(800) 888-4741, *or at www.chicagoreviewpress.com*

CHICAGO REVIEW PRESS

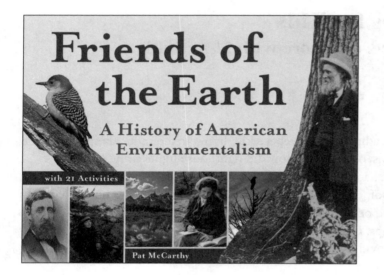

978-1-56976-718-4

$16.95 (CAN $18.95)

Also available in e-book formats

Friends of the Earth
A History of American Environmentalism with 21 Activities

PAT MCCARTHY

The history of American environmentalism is an inspiring story of men and women who dedicated their lives to protecting the nation's natural heritage. Cordelia Stanwood, and later Roger Peterson, revolutionized and popularized birdwatching. Almost singlehandedly, John James Audubon introduced the study of birds in North America, while John Muir pushed a president and a nation into setting aside vast preserves, including Yosemite, Sequoia, Mt. Rainier, and the Grand Canyon. Marjory Stoneman Douglas did the same for the Florida Everglades, as did Mardy Murie with the Grand Tetons and the Arctic National Wildlife Refuge. And Rachel Carson opened the world's eyes to the dangers of pesticides.

In addition to its engaging history, *Friends of the Earth* includes a time line of environmental milestones, a list of popular outdoor parks and sites to visit or explore online, and Web resources for further study. Readers will also learn how to put their concerns into action. They'll build two different types of bird feeders, start a compost pile, study the greenhouse effect, make plaster casts of animals' tracks, plant a tree, test for acid rain, and much more.

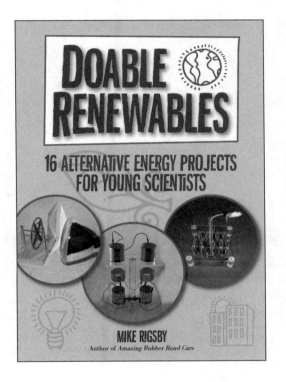

978-1-56976-343-8
$16.95 (CAN $18.95)
Also available in e-book formats

Doable Renewables

16 Alternative Energy Projects for Young Scientists

MIKE RIGSBY

The earth's fossil fuels are being used up at an alarming pace, and once they're gone, they're gone. But other energy sources—solar, wind, waves, "waste" heat, and even human power—are both renewable and environmentally friendly. The projects in this book will help any budding scientist construct and explore working models that generate renewable, alternative energy.

Doable Renewables readers will learn how to build a Kelvin water drop generator out of six recycled cans and alligator clip jumpers, a solar-powered seesaw from a large dial thermometer and a magnifying glass, a windmill from eight yardsticks, PVC pipe, cardboard, and converter generator, and more. They will investigate the energy-generating properties of a solar cell, a radiometer, a Nitinol heat engine, and a Peltier cell. They'll even build a human-powered desk lamp, its energy stored in an array of ultracapacitors. Each project includes a materials and tools list as well as online information on where to find specialized components—a perfect resource for science fair projects.

Available at your favorite bookstore, by calling
(800) 888-4741, or at www.chicagoreviewpress.com

CHICAGO REVIEW PRESS